D0017515

KEYWORDS

KEYWORDS

THE NEW LANGUAGE
OF CAPITALISM

JOHN PATRICK LEARY

Haymarket Books
Chicago, Illinois

© 2018 John Patrick Leary

Published in 2018 by
Haymarket Books
P.O. Box 180165
Chicago, IL 60618
773-583-7884
www.haymarketbooks.org
info@haymarketbooks.org

ISBN: 978-1-60846-962-8

Trade distribution:
In the US, Consortium Book Sales and Distribution, www.cbsd.com
In Canada, Publishers Group Canada, www.pgcbooks.ca
In the UK, Turnaround Publisher Services, www.turnaround-uk.com
All other countries, Ingram Publisher Services International, IPS_Intlsales@ingramcontent.com

This book was published with the generous support of Lannan Foundation and Wallace Action Fund.

Cover design by Josh MacPhee.

Printed in Canada by union labor.

Library of Congress Cataloging-in-Publication data is available.

10 9 8 7 6 5 4 3 2 1

For Louisa,
who already has more grit than all the grifters in all the
world, and who will need it all in the world she inherits.

Any current curse word can become a word of praise, any current truth must inevitably sound to other people as the greatest lie.

Valentin Voloshinov, *Marxism and the Philosophy of Language*

CONTENTS

Language (n.) The music with which we charm the serpents guarding another's treasure.

Ambrose Bierce, *The Devil's Dictionary*

Language, Ambrose Bierce tells us, cannot be trusted, and the sweeter it sounds, the less we should trust it. This is a book about words and their deceptions. The words in this book make up the twenty-first century language of capitalism, a metaphorically rich vernacular in which the defenders of private property speak of virtues and "vision," where wage laborers become imaginative artists and agile athletes, and workplaces are transformed into vibrant ecologies and nurturing communities. In this language, the differences between **creative** resistance to capitalism and creative capitalism, health care and **wellness,** rebellion and **disruption,** and working–class power and the commercial slogan of **empowerment** can be difficult to grasp. These keywords are what Bierce might call charming words used to deprive others of their treasure: if we understood them better, perhaps we might rob them of their seductive power.

Keywords: The New Language of Capitalism is a field guide to the capitalist present, an era of unprecedented technological possibilities to bring humanity together—so we are regularly told, anyway—that also features privation on a scale comparable to

1

Bierce's late nineteenth-century Gilded Age. Are we living in a new stage of capitalism, though, or are today's digital technologies just a different version of our ancestors' railroads and six-shooters, our Silicon Valley titans just the newest update to the ketchup and steel tycoons of an earlier, east-coast fantasy of wealth and opportunity? Identifying what makes our moment unique (or not) is no easy task, in part because we are living in it, and in part because the language we have to understand and describe our era's inequality is itself one of the instruments of perpetuating it. How can we think and act critically in the present when the very medium of the present, language, constantly betrays us?

One way to address this question is to go to the words themselves—to their histories and their present-day semantics. Take **innovation**, today's most popular term for the faith in perpetual improvement that in Bierce's day would have been called "progress." Long before it was any of the many things it is now taken to be—"the **entrepreneurial** function," an elusive quality of successful organizations, the objective of the American educational system—it was widely regarded as a dangerous vice. For centuries, it was condemned as the heresy of conspirators and false prophets—innovators upon the word of God. "In a multitude of men there are many who, supposing themselves wiser than others, endeavour to innovate," Thomas Hobbes wrote in 1651, "and divers Innovators innovate divers wayes, which is a meer distraction, and civill ware." In Shakespeare's Henry IV, the King speaks of "fickle changelings and poor discontents" gaping at the news of "hurly-burly innovation." A century later, Edmund Burke thundered that the "innovators" of revolutionary Paris "leave nothing unrent, unrifled, unravaged, or unpolluted with the slime of their filthy offal."[1]

The twentieth century saw a wholesale renovation of innovation's slimy reputation. Its twenty-first century association with computing technology means that it no longer connotes religious zeal like it once did; nor is innovation any longer a prohibited individual *action*, committed by dissidents and heretics. Instead, it is a pragmatic, benevolent *process*, practiced by individuals but also nurtured by organizations and even by nations. Universities, software corporations, toy makers, museums, banks, pharmaceutical corporations, and soap conglomerates all claim to cultivate and pursue innovation. In the United States government, the importance and goodness of innovation is an issue of bipartisan consensus—embraced with equal alacrity by both the Obama and Trump administrations.

Despite this mainstream acceptance and its current association with technology, innovation retains some of its old link to rebellion and prophecy, as the term's use in the business media and popular advertising shows. "Break rules and dream" is "rule #1" of Silicon Valley's "**ecosystem** of innovation," writes one venture capitalist in a column entitled, appropriately enough, "The Seven Commandments of Silicon Valley." The innovators celebrated in mainstream politics and business are revolutionaries in skinny jeans, visionary personalities whose brilliance can, by some alchemy, be cultivated and reproduced by the same bureaucracies that, we often simultaneously think, tend to stifle idiosyncratic brilliance. This paradoxical combination of heroic anti-orthodoxy and process-driven orthodoxy makes innovation a virtue of a contradictory age. We live in an era in which an apocalyptic imagination holds sway in our cinemas, television shows, video games, and political campaigns, when the slow-motion disasters of debt and climate change imperil the futures of an entire generation of young people around the world. But it is also a historical moment distinguished, especially in the United States, by a powerful elite's faith in the power of technology, and the innovators who wield it, to overcome almost any obstacle. Complex social problems borne of inequality can be solved with technical **solutions**, and if you learn the skills to master a hyper-competitive economy, you can make it. "Need a job? Invent one," suggests Thomas Friedman, that reliable transcriber of ruling-class hobbyhorses, in one of his *New York Times* columns. In a world and an economy rent and ravaged by other people's innovations, the lesson seems to be that you can, and must, creatively fend for yourself. Hobbes might have called this state of affairs "the war of all against all"; we just call it "innovation" and "entrepreneurship."[2]

Keywords: The New Language of Capitalism uses the vocabulary of contemporary capitalism to chronicle this state of affairs and the culture of moralistic exhortation that conditions our responses to it as workers, students, citizens, and consumers. From Silicon Valley to the White House, from kindergarten to college, and from the factory floor to the church pulpit, we are all called to be entrepreneurs and **leaders**, to be **curators** of an ever-expanding roster of **competencies**. Like innovation, many of these words have a secret history that informs their modern usage in surprising ways. Others, like **best practices** and **human capital**, are relatively new coinages that teach us to thrive by applying the lessons of a competitive **marketplace** to every sphere of life. And they all model a kind of ideal personality: someone who is indefatigable, restless, and flexible, always ready to accommodate the shocks of the global economy and the more mundane disruptions of working life, from unpredictable scheduling in service work to reduced parental leave and the outsourcing of more and more administrative tasks to fewer and fewer employees. These keywords share an affinity for hierarchy and competition, an often-uncritical acceptance of the benevolence of computing technologies, and a celebration of moral values thought to be indistinguishable from economic ones: decisive leadership, artistic **passion**, and self-realization. Wealth and professional success are consequences not of fortunate birth, dumb luck, or exploitation, but hard work, "hustle," and **grit**. Because the words in this book have successfully infiltrated everyday life in the United States and elsewhere in the English-speaking world, their meanings often seem self-evident. Uncovering the history and false promises of the language of contemporary capitalism is the objective of this book.

WHAT'S IN A WORD?

A keyword, according to the *Oxford English Dictionary* (hereafer the *OED*), is "a word serving as a key to a cipher or the like." In his 1976 classic *Keywords: A Vocabulary of Culture and Society*, the Welsh literary critic Raymond Williams laid out the foundational vocabulary of modern British society in a wide-ranging project of critical historical semantics. He defined keywords as "binding words in certain activities and their interpretation," elements of a living vocabulary that shape and reflect a society in movement. Keywords show what knowledge ties this society together, and how this common knowledge changes over time. As both Williams and the *OED* make clear, keywords are therefore "key" in a double sense: they are important, and they unlock something hidden. One of the most important of Williams's keywords, "hegemony," is an example of his thesis. As he defines it, "hegemony" shows us how the interests of a ruling class become the commonsense of others. Hegemony, he argues, comes to "depend for its hold not only on its expression of the interests of a ruling class but also on its acceptance as 'normal reality' or 'commonsense' by those in practice subordinated to it."[3] Williams's point about hegemony in particular can be expanded to apply to most of his keywords and mine. That is, the critical study of language and its use can show us not just what a dominant worldview is, but *how* that worldview comes to feel like "normal reality." Many of the books inspired by Williams's project have, like this one, refined or broadened his original lexicon in various ways—for example, to focus on the keywords of a particular field of study, or to expand his roster of terms beyond the reference points of the British left of the mid-1970s. But for the most part, his chosen words are distinguished by their staying power.[4] "Tradition," "culture," "humanity," and "community" are not going anywhere, even as their meanings and uses have changed over time. The words in my collection are generally more specific to the contemporary political moment. They can also be understood as blockages—that is, they are the words we use when we aren't calling things by their proper name. Williams's collection has "management" and "labor"; this one has "leadership" and "human capital."

Many of the words to follow come from what we might broadly describe as "office work," whether it is the language used by the human-resources manager, the aspirational "founder," or the white-collar proletarian whose clerical labors make the office go. This selection may reflect a professional bias on my part: I first encountered many of the words in this collection through my own white-collar job as an English professor in a midwestern public university, a circumstance that may also explain the number of education examples in the pages to follow. However, the managerial tenor of the terms in this book also reflects the way that capitalist ideology renders labor invisible, just as it has always done. It also makes hard, underpaid, repetitious, and insecure work seem palatable by framing it as intellectual, under the sign of what is often called a "knowledge" economy driven by individual cognitive skills like creativity. The keywords of contemporary capitalism fall into four broad categories. The first category we can call late-capitalist body talk. These are words like **brand, flexible, nimble, lean**, and **robust**, which draw on the human body as a metaphor for the corporation—itself already a bodily metaphor, deriving from the Latin *corpus*, or "body"— and which, in turn, frame our labors as an athletic contest governed by fair and transparent rules. Another group exemplifies the moral vocabulary of late capitalism, which as we shall see often draws on religious forebears to justify itself: the enigmatic virtues of innovation, entrepreneurship, **resilience,** passion, and human capital assure us that economic success is nothing less than a moral virtue. A third, related category describes the aesthetics of late capitalism, which posits the artist or craftsperson as a model for the modern worker: **artisanal, collaboration, creativity, curator,** and **maker** fit this bill. This category reflects the influence of what Luc Boltanski and Eve Chiapello call the "artistic critique" of capitalism, and its appropriation by capitalists themselves. Emerging out of the counterculture of the 1960s, which derided the inauthenticity of work under capitalism, the artistic critique of capitalism demanded autonomy, purpose, and transgression—things that workers are now counselled to seek in their jobs. Finally, the fourth category, which deals with the possibilities of technology, includes words like **data** and **hack**, words often used to signal to us that we live in a world with "more possibilities than there's ever been," as a recent credit card commercial bewilderingly claimed. These categories obviously overlap. Many of the bodily metaphors call upon workers' physical *and* moral strength. Economic uses of creativity draw upon that word's link to moral character and artistic work, and privatized social media platforms are usually advertised as ways of bringing people together.[5]

One feature these terms all share is their broad circulation both in mass media and in specialist discussions of working life and the economy. That is, they are not "buzzwords," which I take to be novel, often disposable coinages whose ideological content may be easier to detect and which, therefore, do not infiltrate "normal reality" as insidiously. Nor is this a simple catalog of office jargon, for this reason and one other—while many of these words might slide most readily from the lips of a management consultant, they describe practices of surveillance and labor discipline that also shape assembly-line work, retail jobs, so-called **sharing**-economy gigs, and even life outside of work. **Lean**, for example, originated in automobile manufacturing, and so-called flexible scheduling organizes working life for retail employees. Terms like "personal brand" are used to express managerial power, but they also belong to the language of middle-class striving and fear, sold as a kind of security to office workers vulnerable to outsourcing and layoffs. And while many of these keywords are disseminated from comfortable perches at the *Wall Street Journal* or the *Harvard Business Review,* they are also at home among liberal politicians, idealist students, artists, and NGO directors. The meaning of some terms, like innovation or collaboration, may seem innocuous, the value of creativity and sharing self-evident, the worthiness of **choice** and **smart** unquestionable. Who, after all, would prefer fewer choices or a dumber mobile phone? But this is how the penetration of market discipline into the most quotidian aspects of our everyday lives comes to feel normal. For working adults and young children, at home, at school, at play, and even in church, we are called at all times to be at work building an entrepreneurial self ready to face a world that has little place for an increasing number of us.

The Soviet linguist Valentin Voloshinov, whose 1929 work *Marxism and the Philosophy of Language* was an important source for Williams's study, regarded language as a terrain of social conflict in which it is an ideological battlefield as well as an archive of past political struggles. Writing of the dynamism and vitality of language—what he calls its "multi-accentuality"—Voloshinov describes the way our everyday speech collects the meanings of other speakers, or "social accents," in our own moment and in previous generations. According to Voloshinov, the speakers of a dominant, authoritative accent compete with other overlooked, misunderstood, or silenced voices. Some accents may fade and be forgotten as they give way to new usages, he wrote, but "inasmuch as they are remembered by the philologist and the historian, they may be said to retain the last glimmers of life."[6] Obviously, "glimmers of life" and unheard social accents take us into somewhat speculative territory. The essays that follow are examples of historically-minded literary interpretation, rather than empirical documentation or formal linguistics. I make no claims to the "actual" persistence, whatever that might mean, of innovation's formerly theological accents in its new economic meaning, nor of the glimmers of the Catholic martyr's passion that haunt the word's present-day use to describe a thorough commitment to work. All I can say is that I hear them.

A word on my sources: the definitions, etymological data, and examples of usage in the *Oxford English Dictionary* make it the indispensable resource for any student of the English language, and each of these essays relies upon it. Google's ngram database of printed books has allowed me to visualize broad trends in word usage and popularity. The *Corpus of Contemporary American English* and the *Corpus of Historical American English*, developed by

Mark Davies at Brigham Young University and hosted at https://corpus.byu.edu, allow users to trace developments in the frequency and usage of words in print. For business usage, publications like *Forbes.com* and the *Harvard Business Review* are reliable sources. Outside of the business press, I rely on the archive of the *New York Times* for much of the popular journalistic usage I trace here, given that the paper of record is a good source of the "general predominance which includes, as one of its key features, a particular way of seeing the world and human nature and relationships," as Williams described hegemony. It should go without saying that none of these data sources are politically neutral or foolproof. Like all technologies and archives, they reflect the biases and blind spots of their designers. They may also give this project an American bias, and they don't capture much of spoken and colloquial English. However, taken together they bring out the dominant accents that belong to the words that follow.

WHAT'S NEW ABOUT THE NEW LANGUAGE OF CAPITALISM?

A notable feature of contemporary capitalist discourse is its embrace of what earlier ruling classes never hesitated to repress: dissent and heterodoxy, the stuff of innovation in the old, seventeenth-century sense. And one place where the dominant values of working life are reproduced and contested is in school, which makes education a worthwhile place to consider what, if anything, is distinctive about capitalist culture today. Entrepreneurship (and relatedly, **design** and innovation) is more and more common as a subject and organizing principle of curricula from primary school to college. Partisans of "entrepreneurship education" define entrepreneurship as "the capacity to not only start companies but also to think creatively and ambitiously." Developing these different capacities is the teacher's role. "Entrepreneurship education benefits students from all socioeconomic backgrounds," write Florina Rodov and Sabrina Truong in *Entrepreneur* magazine, "because it teaches kids to think outside the box and nurtures unconventional talents and skills." What is striking here is how, in defining "entrepreneurship," the authors feel no obligation to defend it. It is not that the skills of business strategy or accounting are merely useful things for interested students to learn. Rather, schools should teach entrepreneurship for the same reasons they should nourish the civic and personal values of equality and curiosity. WeWork, a real estate firm that rents out shared office space to aspiring business owners, plans to start a private elementary school, called WeGrow, to teach what it calls "conscious entrepreneurship"—the adjective suggesting that some nebulous sense of social purpose, rather than simple profit, is the pedagogical goal. In an interview, Rebekah Neumann, a WeGrow founder, lamented that most schools crush "the entrepreneurial spirit and creativity that's intrinsic to all young children." She thus treats entrepreneurship as not only a trait that can be associated *with* youthful imagination, creativity, and curiosity, but one that is actually identical with them.[7]

Neumann's sketch of the school's curriculum is as shallow as one would expect of a real-estate charlatan moonlighting in education reform. She refers to a grab-bag of class-bound taste markers—yoga, meditation, farmer's markets where the children will work shifts—details that do little other than signal her private school's target demographic. Schools like WeWork are ultimately invested in reproducing a kind of ideal personality suited to the alternately dystopian and Pollyanna-ish mindset of today's US elite: an autonomous individual entrepreneur built from kindergarten, whose potential can only be realized in the struggle for wealth accumulation, and whose creativity can only be productively exercised for profit. The keyword entrepreneurship here is an example of the bleak moral tenor of today's capitalist common sense: its ideologues are preoccupied with intrinsic "values," but these values are basically mercantile. At the same time, though, it is easy to overstate the novelty of this state of affairs: while WeWork's instrumental notion of learning is stunningly crass, all that is solid has been melting into air for at least a century and a half now. And child labor is certainly nothing new—though it's not even clear whether WeWork students will keep their own wages while staffing their farmer's markets. When Marx and Engels wrote of capitalism's conquest of social relations in the *Communist Manifesto*, they were diagnosing its relentless drive to expand across boundaries both territorial *and* spiritual; the latter conquest is one way to understand WeWork's impulse to monetize children's imaginations. And entrepreneurial education programs are simply doing what common schools have always done: making an era's model workers. So, what makes our moment special?

One way to answer this question is to say, not much. A basic principle of entrepreneurship education is the celebration of economic drives as innate. One of the most famous expressions of this principle is Adam Smith's argument in *The Wealth of Nations* about the human propensity to "truck, barter, and exchange." And a century and a half later in *The Protestant Ethic and the Spirit of Capitalism*, Max Weber famously showed how capitalists in the early American republic succeeded in reclaiming profiteering activities that were once thought unseemly as an "ethos"—the honest fulfillment of a virtuous duty rather than the acquisitive pursuit of private gain. Because capitalism made such a break with tradition, Weber wrote, the "orientation towards profit" required the justification that the religious idea of a "calling" or vocation could provide.[8] The conviction that the way to wealth lies in cultivating one's moral character has inspired self-help literature from Benjamin Franklin, whose autobiography was one of Weber's major sources, down to his twentieth- and twenty-first century descendants, like Dale Carnegie, Stephen Covey, Clayton Christensen, and Angela Duckworth. Here it is useful to remember a point Williams makes about the importance of studying language change. Language is not merely a passive reflection of things as they are, but also a tool for imagining and making things as they could be. Some terms in this book, like creativity, seem to have been with us forever, giving their recent application to primary schooling and urban economic development the air of natural destiny. On the other hand, Williams insists, "new kinds of relationships, but also new ways of seeing existing relationships, appear in language in a variety of ways," as in new coinages like best practices or in the new meanings taken on by older terms like innovation.[9] This movement between tradition and novelty can be seen in individual keywords in this volume. Best practices, for example, seems like a new idea, but remaking institutions in the image of capital, as this term asks us to do, is as old as capitalism. Meanwhile, creativity seems eternal (it's not; its first example in the *OED* dates to 1875), and yet the "creative class" is a very new concept. The supposed timelessness of creativity, though, is key to the concept of the creative class, which derives much of its authority from that timelessness. In short, language can be a historical index that shows us what has and really hasn't changed. In spite of the ideal of constant progress so cherished by market ideologues, the challenges we face are in many ways not so unique. But some real changes, Williams adds, occur within language itself, as in the business class's recent embrace of an acquisitive model of creativity. In each of the words to follow, we will see examples of new terms (and new technologies) recapitulating old conflicts, fears, and ideals. New terms, however, reshape our relationships to these conflicts, fears, and ideals, hiding some older meanings and creating other new ones.

This dynamic of continuity and change raises the thorny question of what term to use to name our contemporary economic moment. Do we live in the era of "late capitalism," a phrase that indicates continuity with previous capitalisms, or are we living under "neoliberalism," a term whose prefix seems to invest our era with a novelty born of a historical break? Now that "socialism" can be more proudly embraced by an English-speaking left a generation removed from the Cold War, the word "capitalism" can be more loudly spoken as well. In this context, "late capitalism" has experienced something of a revival. This term was introduced in 1972 to thinkers on the left by the Marxist economic historian Ernest Mandel to describe the post-war era of economic growth in global capitalism. He insisted that late capitalism was not a wholly new epoch; it was, rather, "merely a further development of the imperialist, monopoly-capitalist epoch," one characterized in part by a "belief in the omnipotence of technology" and the wisdom of experts. Fredric Jameson later popularized "late capitalism" in academic cultural studies in his 1990 classic *Postmodernism: or, the Cultural Logic of Late Capitalism*, where he argued that late capitalism was distinguished by "a prodigious expansion of capital into hitherto uncommodified areas," not only geographical but cultural and spiritual. Jameson acknowledged that it was an imperfect term, an attempt to name what, with different political implications, others have termed postindustrial capitalism, globalization, the knowledge economy, financialization, post-Fordism, and neoliberalism, among other names. The potential capaciousness of the term, which can describe economic shifts as well as their cultural effects, can cause it to be used rather promiscuously. Annie Lowrey calls late capitalism "a catchall phrase for the indignities and absurdities of our contemporary economy." (Uber? That's late capitalism. Uber, but for fill-in-the-blank? Also late capitalism; *Teen Bo$$*, a kind of *Fortune*-meets-*Teenbeat* magazine for teen girl entrepreneurs? Definitely late capitalism. And so on.)[10]

"Neoliberalism" is sometimes used in a similar shorthand way—basically, to name everything bad about the contemporary world—and there is considerable disagreement about the term's meaning and scope. Some dismiss it as leftist jargon, meaningful in too many different ways to be useful.[11] David Harvey defines it rather succinctly, though, as "a theory of political economic practices that proposes that human well-being can best be advanced by liberating individual entrepreneurial freedoms and skills within an institutional framework characterized by strong private property rights, free markets, and free trade," all of which are to be enforced by a strong state. Quinn Slobodian's recent intellectual history of neoliberalism has emphasized the project's goals—primarily the "complete protection of private capital rights" from democratic interference—and the importance of "extra-economic" means to secure these rights. These extra-economic means can include, for example, global institutions like the World Trade Organization (WTO), which can override national laws that restrict capital's power. It also includes the fuzzier realms of culture and morality, which as Slobodian observes might help explain the Charles Koch Foundation's recent investments in bankrolling right-wing humanities programs at American universities. It is also the context for the moral tinge of much of the vocabulary in the pages to come: innovation, entrepreneurship, and creativity all describe the extra-economic realms of the spirit requisitioned for the sake of private property. But we can also find "neoliberalism" being used to identify a theoretical tendency in twentieth-century right-wing economic theory, a set of dominant late twentieth-century political practices and politicians (Ronald Reagan and Margaret Thatcher foremost among them) influenced by those theories, the cultural effects of the practices, and the period of history in which all of the above became dominant.[12]

No single term is exactly suited for the many purposes that each have been assigned, and many of Jameson's original complaints about "late capitalism" have since been made about "neoliberalism": it is used too imprecisely; it has a northern bias, since it works much differently in San Salvador than in San Francisco; it is jargony, familiar only to leftist intellectuals; and so on. But as Mandel himself rather wearily wrote in the introduction to a reprint of his book, "what is really important is not to name, but to explain the historical development that has occurred in our age." And because most arguments about "correct" usages derive from what Williams called "a sacral attitude to words" as they are thought to *be* rather than a critical attitude toward language as people *use* it, calls by some thinkers on the left for "neoliberalism" to be retired in favor of one term or another strike me as more pointless than wrong. I generally avoid the term "neoliberalism" in this book, though, because I do not engage at length with the work of neoliberals like conservative twentieth-century economic theorists Friedrich Hayek, Milton Friedman, or Ludwig von Mises. I also want to emphasize a point Mandel and

Jameson make, that "late capitalism" is only the *latest* form of an old system.[13] In this book, we will see that *contra* the euphoric claims of innovators or the apocalyptic claims of some of their critics, things now are different, but also very much the same. In other words: to those fearful that neoliberalism is swallowing humanity, cheer up: things have always been terrible![14]

THE COLD COMFORTS OF LATE CAPITALISM

The neoliberals' attention to the extra-economic realms of art, morality, and the self is especially important. Terms germane to the contemporary office, like creativity, take on new meaning in the 1960s, especially in the organizational psychology associated with Abraham Maslow and others, which counselled workers to seek personal fulfillment at work. Other terms, like smart and maker, are closely linked to the internet but have roots in older ideologies of technology and aesthetics. Still others, like human capital, treat a financial appraisal of oneself and others as a natural human inclination, and even a liberatory one. This only becomes commonsensical, though, after the early 1970s, when the economies of the Global North moved away from manufacturing and toward the management and manipulation of risk. And before the abolition of slavery, of course, human capital would have meant something quite different. The reduction of everyday social relations to exercises in risk management is distressing, to say the least, in ways that critics have discussed. But instead of emphasizing all the good things that late capitalism (or neoliberalism, if you prefer) confiscates, I am also convinced by Leigh Claire La Berge and Slobodian's argument that a plausible critique of neoliberalism (the term they use) must also take seriously what it purports to offer: what "meanings, life stories . . . and affects" neoliberalism makes possible for us, even if they are hollow gifts. Indeed, in focusing on the language of capitalism, we must grapple with the sense of possibility this language promises: a keyword wouldn't become *key*, after all, if it were simply a record of horrors.

In his book *Financialization of Daily Life*, the scholar Randy Martin called the life-cycle produced by such a system a "financially leavened existence," a phrase that elegantly captures the puffy vacuity of so much innovation discourse, but which also reminds us how much we are all nourished by it. A financially leavened existence tells us that the debts we owe and the work we do for others—often increasingly low-paid and casual—are "investments in ourselves," sure to pay off later. As an example, in a news article about an "innovation arms race" at elite US universities—a building and spending boom on so-called entrepreneurship centers purporting to train students for lucrative business careers—one student reflected on the opportunity that springs from the stagnant job market she and her cohort face after graduation. She framed this worrisome circumstance in surprisingly upbeat terms: for her, job insecurity is almost a generational virtue, a willingness to not only pull yourself up by your own bootstraps, but to do so repeatedly. "To be honest, our generation is no longer interested in doing one thing for the rest of our lives," the student said. "Our generation is interested in learning different things, and if the environment does not provide it, we want to jump out and take a risk."[15] Nurturing an entrepreneurial self becomes not a self-abnegating and exhausting sacrifice here, but a source of possibility. In this way, the ideal of entrepreneurial selfhood spins the old straw of bootstraps individualism into something that shines like gold.

This student uses "risk" in the common colloquial sense—to describe a chance one takes on something—but she also is using it in a financial sense, as the chance that an investment return will be lower than expected. Here, though, "the investment" is her working life, and while it's clear that she bears the risk of insecure employment, it's not clear that she is the one managing that risk. Here, in the blurred nuances of this word risk, we can see an example of Martin's claim that financial capitalism compels us to "merge the business and life cycles"—to harmonize one's "work-life balance," to put it in the favored terms of economic journalism. But as described by the student above, this task is not a burden to be borne, but an opportunity to be seized. Relentlessly busy, visionary, and creatively enterprising, speculating upon the future appreciation of one's present (educational and material) assets, the financially leavened-self treats work as a way to pursue one's purpose. Work as labor—exhausting, exploitative, but performed with and for others—fades into the background of work as the acquisition of self. Whether one is an actor, insurance adjuster, college professor, or barista, the key to making your day job something more than drudgery— the way to make it your "life's work"—is to embrace it as your passion. The idea of a passionate commitment *to* labor can create widely mocked grotesqueries like the 2016 Lyft advertisement that celebrated a pregnant driver who completed fares while she was going *into* labor (the company then creepily welcomed the woman's newborn daughter "to the Lyft family"). The pursuit of resistance to work through an identification *with* it might sound especially awful in these cases, but in many others, it is undeniably seductive—the college professor who writes these very lines on a weekend evening must admit to being a sucker for it. The advantage of this sense of self in a world characterized by apocalyptic anxieties and deep inequality is some sense of control over the future and some sense of justice in the present. If you are **failing**, this is only in the service of maximizing future success; if you are "succeeding," then congratulations, you earned it.[16]

Weber argued in *The Protestant Ethic and the Spirit of Capitalism* that when capitalist culture treated the pursuit of wealth as a virtuous ethos, it provided a moral justification that the system required. In a post-Communist world in which capitalism has triumphed almost everywhere, it might seem that there is no more need for justifications. But, in our time, capitalism is under increasing pressure, and its newest justifications frame the global rule of the market as the source of freedom: no longer just to vote against Communist governments, but to pursue more fundamental desires—for beauty, community, and a sense of purpose. Hence the WeWork academy's emphasis on entrepreneurship's inner glow and the idealization in business literature of makers, artisans, and other creative types who were once more often set against the rhythms and routines of factory and office life. The unorthodox artist is no longer an enemy of the buttoned-up white-collar office, for example; she is supposed to be at home there. It also explains the popularity in business discourse of concepts loosely associated with rebellion (like disruption) words for nonprofit activities (like curation), or terms actually appropriated from the left (like empowerment). The need to cultivate a personal brand would have been unintelligible to people a generation ago, for whom brands only existed on cans of soup or the skin of chattel. Our predicament is therefore different and arguably more severe than the one faced by Weber: not only have our private creative aspirations and spiritual lives been appropriated *by* the market, they are held to be its most dynamic sources. Weber's "orientation towards profit" no longer requires justification as a calling or a spirit; for some, it is practically human nature.

The internalization of the will to profit as an intrinsic human trait, and a righteous one at that, gives the vocabulary of late capitalism a combination of moral aridity and euphoric optimism that can be as bewildering as it is depressing. The dispiriting prospect of kindergarteners writing business plans reminds us of an important metaphor in Williams' definition of keywords: they are "binding" words, a term Williams uses to describe the language that holds a society and its ideas together, shaping the consensus of an era or a community. Innovation and entrepreneurship have become such commonsense concepts and so widely accepted as virtues that they often remain undefined by those who use them in earnest. Binding words also *bind* in another sense, as constraints that manacle our imagination. And what is a child's imagination anyway but a bit of idle human capital?

Late capitalism's false promises have been a source of consensus, but they can also be a point of angry renewal, provided we reject them and replace them with something better. Ultimately, my goal is not just to decry neoliberalism's gobbling up of our spiritual and social lives. Though this book emerged out of disgust, I hope these essays can prod readers to reflect upon the keywords of the other world that remains possible. So, for free time, not "flexibility"; for free health care, not "wellness"; and for free universities, not the "marketplace of ideas." For people power, not private "empowerment"; for more masses and fewer "leaders"; for imagination, and not "entrepreneurship"; for solidarity, not "sharing"; and for communal luxury, not solitary "grit." If any of this sounds nostalgic, so be it; better that than the dull "futures" imagined by our culture of techno-fabulists. So, if we must have innovation, let it be the old hurly-burly kind.

ACCOUNTABILITY (N.); ACCOUNTABLE, (ADJ.)

Accountability is a term that has exploded in popularity over the last five decades after remaining relatively consistent for centuries.[1] It shares with **innovation** a deep and mostly forgotten religious background. With the combination of moral responsibility it retains from its Christian origins and the now dominant meaning of task-based "counting," accountability captures the popular fantasy of quantifying virtue. It is popular on both the left and the right in calls for corporate or government accountability. The General Accounting Office, founded in 1921, changed its name in 2004 to the Government Accountability Office (GAO), a subtle shift indicating a significant change in mission. The GAO's original mission was to seek "greater economy or efficiency in public expenditures." Now, replacing "public" with "taxpayer," the GAO investigates "how the federal government spends taxpayer dollars." The new mission, with its emphasis on the private taxpayer over the shared public, captures the hostility to public spending typical of an era of conservative attacks on "big government."[2]

Perhaps its greatest influence has come in the field of US public education reform, especially since the 2002 No Child Left Behind Act. As its law's preamble put it, the NCLB set out "to close the achievement gap with accountability, **flexibility**, and **choice**, so that no child is left behind." The Department of Education explained accountability in 2003 this way:

> Under the act's accountability provisions, states must describe how they will close the achievement gap and make sure all

students, including those who are disadvantaged, achieve academic proficiency. They must produce annual state and school district report cards that inform parents and communities about state and school progress. Schools that do not make progress must provide supplemental services, such as free tutoring or after-school assistance; take corrective actions; and, if still not making adequate yearly progress after five years, make dramatic changes to the way the school is run.[3]

This is a very nearly tautological definition, since it defines "accountability" by means of the mechanisms for being "held accountable." This is an important quality of the term, however: while the concept of "accountability" presumes moral responsibility, the word is defined in terms of the mechanisms of enforcement. This means that, like **stakeholder**, accountability cannot be separated from a bureaucracy's public performance of responsibility—you are accountable to the degree that you can be perceived as being accountable.

Accountability thrives in the management literature where **leaders** justify themselves to each other. What do the scribes of the *Harvard Business Review* see as the biggest fault among leaders today? "No matter how tough a game they may talk about performance," they write, "when it comes to holding people's feet to the fire, leaders step back from the heat." In other words: some leaders fall short in the work of not blaming other people for enough things. Indeed, accountability is a word that, unlike its relative "responsibility," assumes retribution—again, accountability is unthinkable apart from mechanisms of enforcement and punishment. The *OED* defines it as "the liability to account for and answer for one's conduct." So, while one can generally *be responsible*—for your friends, relatives, students, goldfish, etc.—you are only *held accountable*, by someone else, when you have failed. And then there is the question of whom one is liable *to*—the students, in education? The public? The "taxpayer," that parsimonious substitute for the dwindling "public"?[4]

Police accountability, for example, has emerged recently in the United States as a goal of some activists confronting police brutality and mass incarceration. Educational "accountability" is based on the teacher and the school's moral responsibility for the welfare of all children. What gives the concept of "accountability" its political force, therefore, is its claim on justice. To be accountable—that is, for a school to meet the uniform state standards for what the law termed Adequate Yearly Progress—is to be held accountable, that is, to face sanctions for failure. Measurement is key in enforcing the notion of accountability in schools, and it is what many critics of NCLB have fixated on: the high-stakes testing regimes, teacher evaluations, school grades, and the mandate of uniform standards without enough redress of unequal conditions. Accountability takes knowledge quantification as a fundamental principle, as NCLB critic Anthony Cody points out in a reading of a Common Core promotional video.

> Like it or not, life is full of measuring sticks: How smart we are, how fast we are, how we can, you know, compete. But up until now, it's been pretty hard to tell how well kids are competing in school, and how well they're going to do when they get out of school. We like to think that our education system does that. But when it comes to learning what they really need to be successful after graduation, is a girl in your neighborhood being taught as much as her friend over in the next one? Is a graduating senior in, say, St. Louis, as prepared to get a job as a graduate in Shanghai? Well, it turns out the answer to both of these questions is "no."[5]

As Cody argues, this view of education makes several assumptions—that life is a sequence of measuring sticks, and that a child's education must be thought of as one part of an international competition, a zero-sum war-game with Chinese schoolchildren for the jobs of the future.[6]

Accountability, in sum, mandates measurement and standardization in the fields in which it is applied. Of course, measurement and standards are not bad in and of themselves, even in education, defined as it is in the US by gross disparities in local school funding and teacher training. Rather, the problem is the degree to which accountability regimes overlook these structural impediments, given their reliance for data and enforcement on the bureaucracies that produce the metrics. Consider the example of police accountability: as the policing scholar Alex Vitale has argued, accountability measures, like body cameras and civilian complaint boards, are not only subject to the authority of the police—who can turn off the camera or stonewall the board—but also "leave intact the basic institutional functions of the police, which have never really been about public safety or crime control."[7] Accountability is a technocratic ideal of justice, limited by the authority and prerogative of the bureaucracies to which one is held accountable. My own sense, as a teacher, has been that administrators only really begin counting things when they need to justify getting rid of them. When it combines the moral sense of duty with the bureaucratic zeal for quantification, accountability encodes the fiction that moral obligations can be measured, calculated, and, of course, valued financially.

ARTISANAL (ADJ.); ARTISAN (N.)

Artisanal has always been a word with a class meaning. It has long been used in Marxist writing to describe pre-capitalist modes of production, and more broadly forms of labor typically distinguished by prestige and status from "artistic." In the Marxist tradition, the artisan was conventionally understood in terms of a framework of loss—the subjugation of "the previously independent craftsman" and his conversion into a "hired industrial worker" in the rise of European capitalism, as Leon Trotsky explained it. This loss can also be understood in the positive terms of efficiency and speed, as in the rise of mass production at Ford, where cars once slowly and expensively stitched together in a workshop by a team of artisans were quickly and cheaply assembled along a moving line by unskilled laborers. Loss and redemption were points of departure for E. P. Thompson's *The Making of the English Working Class,* the pioneering Marxist history of the English artisan. "I am seeking to rescue the poor stockinger, the Luddite cropper, the "obsolete" hand-loom weaver, the "Uto-

pian" artisan . . . from the enormous condescension of posterity,"
Thompson wrote in his preface. A different mission of reclamation also pervades the recent rise of "artisanal," the adjective, as
a brand identity for a variety of consumer goods made slowly and
by hand, according to methods preserved in folk memory, family
lore, or some other archive. The difference between "artisanal"
and "artisan," though, is the difference between a brand identity and a *class* identity. Artisanal products are generally aimed
at bourgeois consumers; the artisan struggled against bourgeois
producers.[8]

The fashion for artisanal products has a socialist genealogy,
although the proverbial organic apple has fallen rather far from
the tree when we consider today's $80 Japanese denim mechan-
ic's apron. William Morris, the nineteenth-century socialist and
leader of the Arts and Crafts Movement, sought to preserve craft
techniques from destruction by mass production. He is an indi-
rect inspiration to many of today's devotees of artisanal or **maker**
culture, even if the latter term is defined by an enthusiasm for,
rather than a suspicion of, the labor-saving technology that Morris criticized. In one essay, Morris defines "artisan" in terms of
its loss of the intellectual capacity retained by the artist. This
distinction between artisans and artists has long been fundamental to the meaning of each. A seventeenth-century French-Eng-
lish dictionary translated the word "spirit" as the "heart" that
an artisan has in his fingers, rather than his head. "The Ger-
mans," explained its author, "are better Artisans than Artists,
better at handy-crafts then at head-craft." The artist, then, was
an intellectual, developing **creative** work for pleasure and en-
lightenment; the artisan was a craftsman, making products for
some practical use. Morris took aim at this distinction between
hand- and head-craft, which he dates to the "rise of capitalism in
the sixteenth century," before which, he says, all craftsmen who
made anything were artists of some kind. "What we want," he
wrote in "Artists and Artisan as Artist Sees It," "is to extinguish
not the artist, but the mere artisan, by destroying the flattery
craving flunkey in the one, and the brutal toil-worn slave in the

other, so that they may both be men." Raymond Williams, for his part, dates the break between the artist and the artisan much later, to the Royal Academy's exclusion of engravers in the late eighteenth century. The artisan was henceforth a skilled manual laborer, the artist an imaginative creator, and the worker an extension of the machine he works, or rather which works him.[9] Whenever we date the breach between the artist and the artisan, it is a product of a class-stratified society and the kinds of knowledge work such a society values.[10]

There is thus both an economic and a moral dimension to most discussions of the artisan: she or he has been a degraded form of the more honored artist, but also a worker displaced by capitalism, whose work is pulverized by the cheapened baubles of commercial capitalism. It is easy, however, to denounce these baubles without inquiring into the systems that make their production possible and profitable. A survey of the word's recent history in the *New York Times* shows that the adjective "artisanal" has been attached most of all to food, first appearing in articles on European gastronomic traditions—cheese-making, viniculture, etc.—in the early 1980s. The term explodes in popularity after 2000, when it comes to be applied more often to restaurants and food products in the US.[11] Many contemporary American celebrations of the food artisan emphasize, quite understandably, the degradation of the country's regional and cultural foodways under corporate agriculture and processed food production—think of how many people have never eaten fried chicken outside a KFC, never tasted a homemade pickle, or never eaten macaroni and cheese that was not orange. But critiques of consumption practices that ignore the class privilege that would enable healthier and more diverse food choices (and would support a reader's interest in midtown Manhattan *fromageries*) commit the old error that Marx attributed to the anarchist Michel Proudhon, who mourned the relative independence of the artisan class as it was disappearing in the latter half of the nineteenth century. In *The Poverty of Philosophy,* Marx charged that Proudhon insisted on seeing the factory machines themselves as the culprit of the artisan's downfall, rather than the economic relation of labor to capital, of which the machines' dominance over artisanal skill was only a symptom. Later, the Morris-inspired Arts and Crafts Movement, as Jackson Lears has written, responded to regimentation and inequality in modern industry by reviving old methods of craft production. By attempting to restore to the worker the autonomy the factory had taken away, the movement would also provide consumers with the beauty they were missing. But without structural reforms of the economic system, the Arts and Crafts Movement, which aimed to liberate workers, became a niche market for middle-class buyers. Thus it is with artisanal consumption today.[12]

BEST PRACTICES (N. PL.)

The term best practices was popularized by Robert Camp's 1989 book *Benchmarking: The Search for Industry Best Practices that Lead to Superior Performance,* which used it to mean a broadly applicable standard for **excellence** in any field. From its origins in the business press, it has migrated into elementary to higher education, nonprofit fields, and politics, where it suggests **solution**-oriented practicality. Like most jargon, the meaning of best practices comes as much from its literal signification as from the belonging that its use indicates: by using the phrase, one signals one's place in a professional class and one's knowledge of its attendant ideas.

The parent concept of best practices is "benchmarking," which Camp defines as "the search for those best practices that will lead to the superior performance of a company," and the pursuit of a standard of performance that "removes the subjectivity from decision-making." Benchmarking's derivation from mechanical trades—Camp notes the term's origins as the surveyor's standard reference mark—helps to give best practices its sense of objectivity and practicality. And as its superlative construction suggests, "best" practices are concerned with superiority. Writing in the 1980s, Camp frames his book as an explanation of the methods by which Japanese business has gained a competitive advantage over the United States. In explaining his definition, he uses a Japanese word, "dantotsu," which he translates as "the best of the best practices, best of class, best of breed." We lack a single such word in English, Camp surmises, perhaps because

Americans (and, presumably, the English, New Zealanders, etc.) always assumed they were the best. "We cannot assume anything anymore," he warns. "Benchmarking moves us past that assumption." Best practices, then, are neutral and independent of narrow national or professional prejudices—one searches for the best ways to do a thing regardless of where one finds them. We might conclude two things from all this: first, the term best practices indicates the same combination of optimism and fear that also motivates **innovation.** Despite its pragmatic positivity, the turn to best practices is motivated by anxiety about national decline. In the United States, because of what Camp correctly diagnoses as a widespread tendency toward jingoism, it is difficult to assimilate foreign competition and domestic job loss into the national narrative of progress. Part of the appeal of best practices lies in the antiseptic technicality with which it dispatches these fears. An organization pursuing best practices endeavors to follow what one encyclopedia calls "the most efficient or prudent course of action," which makes it admittedly hard to argue with. What teacher, banker, crossing guard, or bus driver doesn't want that? What alternative could there be—merely fine practices?[1]

The problem, as Wendy Brown shows in her book *Undoing the Demos,* lies in the way that best practices separates "practices" from "products." As she argues, value inheres in "practices," which are thought to be portable (with some customization, of course) from one field or organization to the next. Just like solutions, best practices emphasizes problem-solving. But because the term derives from the business world, where market competitiveness is the value that separates "best" practices from deficient ones, the sense of quality that inheres in the concept is typically **market**-based. This is where its alleged neutrality begins to fray. Of the principal consultants named in late 2017 on the website of Entangled Solutions—an "innovation agency for education" that offers clients at the University of California services like "best practices analysis"—five held an MBA, three claimed experience in higher education administration, and only one had university teaching experience outside of a business school. As

Brown argues, the phrase best practices carries two complementary meanings. First, the term describes a basically market-based (i.e., profit-driven) standard of evaluation, which organizes how we think about public services like public higher education. Additionally, best practices imbues actual profit-driven organizations with the public **accountability** that the public sector is supposed to provide. Because best practices incorporates ethics and accountability into its logic, it implies a kind of self-regulation: why regulate a corporation when its best practices already require it to act ethically?[2]

To take another example: in 2016, news broke that the residents of Flint, MI had been exposed to lead-contaminated water for nearly two years. The city's state-appointed emergency manager was charged with pursuing cost-efficiency in public services—including the municipal water supply. Public health, which costs money, predictably suffered. In response, Michigan's Republican Governor Rick Snyder, a former executive whose love of business jargon is boundless, promised to fix it with a "best practices approach for individual locations with water lead levels greater than 15 ppb," considered a baseline rate of toxicity. But it was the pursuit of a version of best practices—the privatization of a public utility, running government like a business—that got Flint into its deadly mess. And Snyder counseled a skeptical public that best practices would get it out.

BRAND (N., V.)

Branding's origins in the painful burning of flesh have never totally left the word's usages. While branding has always been a mark of property ownership, the major transformation in the word's usage from the nineteenth to the mid-twentieth century was transfer of the brand's possession from proprietor, the owner of the brand applied to chattel to consumer, the buyer of a "brand-name" product. The use of brands to describe particular varieties of domestic consumer goods at the beginning of the twentieth century marked its initial appearance in our vocabulary as something other than a mark of ownership on livestock. The twenty-first century has seen one more transformation: you don't just consume brands, you can become one yourself.

Before the late nineteenth century, "brand" was a word most often encountered as a transitive verb, as in "to brand cattle." It was (and still is) the direct, searing application of proof of ownership by the owner of land and chattel. The average consumer became the owner of branded objects between the late nineteenth century, when modern consumer branding makes its fitful start, and the middle of the twentieth. Then, brands were still a designation of uniqueness, but this designation had become less of a literal denotation of *property* and more of a symbolic connotation of *quality*. Hence the once popular and now quaint adjective "brand-name," used to distinguish a product from the generic store variety. Branding in this sense was a metaphor that drew on the original mark of ownership, but the supermarket brand connected symbolic associations to everyday products—retaining the prestige of ownership while losing the material referent of its initial use as hot iron on living flesh.

Other metaphorical uses of the verb "to brand" remained widespread in the nineteenth and early twentieth centuries, but its use was widely negative. One of the most common such usages can be seen in constructions like to "brand a coward" or "brand a liar." Now, branding suggests the transcendence of the mere object—we can all easily recognize, for example, how Jif Peanut Butter represents not just peanuts ground into a tasty paste, but maternal love itself. What's been lost, therefore, is the sense of humiliation that comes with being marked as a fraud or a sinner or possessed as a slave and an object. Now, to brand a person, a nonprofit institution, or an idea is, paradoxically, to elevate it beyond its material existence, rather than debase it by reducing it to the same.

Consider the concept of the "political brand." A course in political marketing at the University of Auckland in New Zealand advertises itself with Warhol-inspired soup cans emblazoned with political brand associations like "change," "hope," and "progress." "Whereas a product has distinct functional parts such as a politician and policy," reads the course description, "a brand is intangible and psychological. A political brand is the overarching feeling, impression, association or image the public has towards a politician, political organization, or nation." The phrase "political brand" goes back a long way, but until quite recently it was always used in the sense of "brand's" mid-century consumer use—as a synonym for a "variety," as in "Roosevelt's Democratic brand of government." In the Cold War, it was used disparagingly, as a synonym of "variety" tinged with the moral sense of disrepute: Tito's or Castro's "brand of Communism," for example. Today, one typically hears political brand in the way the Auckland politics professor means it: neither as a symbol of the product, nor a synonym for its distinctiveness, nor a mark of deceit, but as the political "product" itself. In the *New York Times*, the phrase "political brand" only became common during the 2004 US presidential campaign, but it is ubiquitous in US political discourse now. In 2015, Rep. G. K. Butterfield, a North Carolina Democrat and chair of the Congressional Black Caucus, described his disappointment with his Republican colleagues' failure to observe the fiftieth anniversary of the Selma, AL, civil rights march: "the Republicans always talk about trying to change their brand and be more appealing to minority folks," he said disapprovingly.[3] What's notable about this usage is that Butterfield's disapproval is not meant cynically, as if a political "rebranding" of racist politics was an insincere gesture to disguise a reactionary spirit. He's sincere about the "Republican brand" as a meaningful expression of the Republican spirit.

The tense and aspect of the verb "to brand" as it is conventionally used are also important. A rebranding is continuous: either one "re-brands" or is in the act of "branding," just as the Republicans in the example above are "trying to change their brand." The past tense of the verb is less often used, since to do so would presumably reveal either a failure to successfully rebrand or, if successful, the fraudulence of the enterprise. The verb thus manifests a curious combination of searing permanence and constant reinvention. This painful, paradoxical combination permeates the discourse of "personal branding." The personal brand has an origin story and an author: the best-selling management consultant Tom Peters, whose 1997 *Fast Company* article "The Brand Called You" is something of a classic in the executive self-help genre. Peters's conversational, exclamatory prose is the trademark—the brand, if you like—of a master stylist of executive pablum.

> Start right now: as of this moment you're going to think of yourself differently! You're not an "employee" of General Motors, you're not a "staffer" at General Mills, you're not a "worker" at General Electric or a "human resource" at General Dynamics (ooops, it's gone!). Forget the Generals! You don't "belong to" any company for life, and your chief affiliation isn't to any particular "function." You're not defined by your job title and you're not confined by your job description. Starting today you are a brand.

Peters defines the personal brand as an exercise of what it might seem explicitly *not* to be: personal authenticity and autonomy. Against the job descriptions and tropes of mid-twentieth-century executive selfhood, against the mammoth "Generals" and the stability they promised, Peters offers an upbeat account of job insecurity that plays on old American ideals of reinvention. Precarious employment is merely an opportunity to light out for the territory. Branding at mid-century, Naomi Klein writes in *No Logo*, was "hawking product"; today, in the work of Peters and those he inspired, it offers what she calls "corporate transcendence."[4] With his citations of clichés of heroic American self-making—Thoreau, Whitman, the Marlboro Man, etc.—Peters reminds his readers that they are not products. They are free-born individuals with limitless potential. They are, in other words, brands.

For Peters, one's renewable personal brand is really a professional brand, of course, but the logic of personal branding denies that there is a difference. The cost of this autonomy, though, is constant work and self-scrutiny. Meanwhile, service workers, hidden behind their "branded" aprons and ballcaps, are more or less invisible. Despite the relative prestige of the personal brand discourse, it is hard to avoid reading Peters's trademark enthusiasm as a manifestation of a much deeper anxiety. As the management theorists Daniel Lair, Katie Sullivan, and George Cheney have recently argued, the "turbulence" of contemporary capitalism is often misapprehended as a problem only of communication: one's failure to get along is a failure to acclimate to new technologies, especially new communications media. Branding yourself is a way of acclimating to these new technologies. Communication media, then, is treated as the cause of and solution to the unemployment crisis.[5]

The "personal brand" is thus a concept that celebrates self-commodification, which Klein's book had denounced as a new feature of corporate domination. For the personal branding consultants, it is **empowerment**, an "investment in yourself." In politics and in managerial consulting, what is notable about many contemporary uses of "branding" is an indifference to, and even a seeming unawareness of, the charge of inauthenticity.[6] Indeed, brand "gurus" are embarrassingly glib, their arguments superficial and easily refuted, and the packaging of their ideas often severely inept for people whose expertise purports to be in communication. But the incompetence of personal brand discourse has also been a major part of its appeal. To borrow a similar point Sarah Brouillette makes about the "**creative** class" slogan popularized by Richard Florida, the University of Toronto scholar and consultant, branded ideas like personal branding have an elegant, maddening coherence.[7] All of their ideas about branding are brands themselves: digestible, imitable, applicable, and marketable. This takes us back to branding's older meanings, as both a mark of typicality and a mark of distinction. Indeed, "personal branding" in our day is advertised as a way of living your authentic self—authenticity and its appearance are scarcely distinguishable. Even as it aspires to an unlikely sort of transcendence, though, the brand's familiar origins in the marking of property reminds us of that laboring body whose **flexibility** has psychic and physical limits.

CHOICE (N.)

Many uses of choice in contemporary Anglo-American political discourse tell a story about political and economic power, in which the protagonist is an individual freely weighing options in a rational **marketplace**. Whether we are talking about the private purchase of some consumer good, or describing political decisions made in the voting booth or in a representative chamber, "choice" has become a word used to describe the practice of freedom.

This has a complex intellectual history, but one point of origin is the conservative "public choice" theory developed by the conservative economist James Buchanan at the University of Virginia between the late 1950s and 1960s, who evaluated political decision-making in terms of the decisions made by individual participants in an economic exchange. If markets (a realm of private choices) and governments (the sphere of public ones) are analogous institutional contexts—as Buchanan argued—then participants in each simply try to maximize their individual advantage. What this means, in short, is that there is no public interest—there are only public *choices*. And public choices are always market-based choices, which government officials tend to make to protect their monopoly interest in governing and its funding streams in taxation. As Nancy McLean argues in *Democracy in Chains*, in foregrounding property rights over the public interest in this way, public choice theory lent a modern "moral vocabulary" to a version of political economy that otherwise belonged to the late nineteenth century, when property rights were sacrosanct.[1] Conservatives and liberals alike speak in this vocabulary today when anyone wonders why government cannot be run more like a business, or when its defenders praise the Affordable Care Act (i.e., Obamacare) for facilitating consumers' ability to choose private insurance plans. The question of whether a person might prefer not to choose at all—might prefer, in other words, to simply use one collective health care program—is foreclosed by a debate that regards individual choice as the horizon of political participation. In the way that we typically use the word politically, more choices are always good, even when you are choosing between opaque and expensive contracts on your own sickness.

An advantage that choice enjoys in political rhetoric derives from its adjectival meanings: "select" or "exquisite." Consider the phrase "schools of choice" as it is used in states like Michigan, which has embraced "school choice" policy with abandon. A *school of choice* is a school that accepts pupils who live outside of its local district. A *choice school*, like a choice autumn apple, is thus a sought-after commodity, and the economic argument for school choice is based on this sense of education as a product in a free market. The familiar argument then follows that competition for parents and pupils, like competition for discerning apple consumers, will drive up quality across the board. Many economists would grant that *homo economicus* is often an irrational creature, and most fruit lovers would concede that apples available for sale are more often mealy than they are choice. But in the most ideological uses of the market as a model for social and political life, economic choices are exercises in freedom. Whether you are evaluating breakfast cereals, political candidates, health insurance plans, or charter high schools, the ability to choose is ipso facto the *freedom* to choose, regardless of the conditions that determine the choices one can make—expensiveness of neighborhood fruit markets, miserableness of candidates, complexity of insurance plans, the distance from home of charter schools, and the residential segregation of metropolitan areas.[2]

This celebration of choice as a virtue in and of itself is captured succinctly by Margaret Thatcher. "Choice," she told an audience in 1977, "is the essence of ethics: if there were no choice, there would be no ethics, no good, no evil; good and evil have meaning only insofar as man is free to choose."[3] Individual choice (between, say, private health insurance providers) can be opposed to social responsibility (for a nationalized health system that benefits all). Here, though, Thatcher *conflates* individual choice with social responsibility, as if they are identical.[4] In a society structured around the wisdom of individual consumer choices, there is no such thing as the people, the community, or as Thatcher famously said, society—there are only individuals, whose responsibility is to themselves. And thus, when you are "free" to choose a health plan or your child's charter high school, you become responsible for the results. This freedom is a particularly cynical ruse, since such "choices" quickly become compulsory.

COACH (N., V.)

"Life coaching" is a practice built on metaphor: firstly, the title itself assumes for a professional mentor the qualities of exhortation and strategy-setting linked with the manager of a football or basketball team. And life coaches are themselves enamored of metaphor: those who wait for a magic wand fail to see that they have been the magic wand all along, says Thomas Leonard, patriarch (as he is often called) of life coaching. "My job is to give my clients a tool belt," says another coach. Another favors an exercise involving the metaphor of a hidden box. Visualize your hidden box, imagine what you put inside it, and think about where you hide it, this coach advises—this will allow you to recognize what you are hiding from yourself. By doing so, you can, if you will, think outside of the box.[5]

"Metaphor," as its Greek root tells us, is a "carrying across" of meaning from one concept or object to another. Through a simple turn of phrase, metaphors allow us to formulate one thing—

routine, say, or conventional wisdom—in terms of something qualitatively different, like a box. Life coaching is built around metaphor's rhetorical alchemy, which turns something abstract (psychological repression, your underappreciated talents) into something concrete (a box, a magic wand). Coaching's conjuring act claims to deliver concrete results for clients whose struggles at work may seem abstract, linked as they inevitably are to political and economic forces larger than any individual. In his book *28 Laws of Attraction: Stop Chasing Success and Let It Chase You* (originally published in 1998 as *The Portable Coach*) Leonard counseled readers to "unhook" themselves from the future. The advice is to look inward rather than outward, to focus on today instead of fretting about tomorrow, or as another coach describes the mission, to help clients gain "more access to the brilliance [they] already have." To reverse a popular left-wing slogan, it's not capitalism, it's you.[6]

Life coaching is a relatively recent concept; Leonard founded the International Coach Federation, a trade association, in 1995. The *New York Times* makes an early mention of "life coaches" (in scare quotes) in 1999, and stories from 2008 reported on it as a curious new phenomenon.[7] Despite its novelty, coaching draws on deep wells in the tradition of American self-help. There is, in coaching, much of the "power of positive thinking" (the title of Norman Vincent Peale's famous 1952 book, which advised readers to visualize their success), and there is the emphasis on the cultivation of winning personal habits in and outside of work (the argument of Stephen R. Covey's 1989 *The Seven Habits of Highly Effective People*, who covered similar ground as Dale Carnegie's 1936 classic, *How to Win Friends and Influence People*). Even further back in the American self-help canon is the Philadelphia Baptist minister and Temple University founder Russell Conwell, whose 1890 book *Acres of Diamonds* was a major success in its own era of inequality and massive fortunes. In the story that gives the book its title, which Conwell told and retold to paying audiences around the world, an ambitious man leaves his farm and wanders the world in a futile search for riches, eventually dying, alone and disappointed, on some foreign shore. When the new owner of his old farm digs a well in the backyard, he discovers diamonds (acres of them), and becomes rich beyond his dreams. The lesson is that the ability to get rich is within your grasp, if only you unhook yourself from anxiety about the future or, to use Conwell's preferred metaphor, look in your own figurative backyard. Conwell spoke in a language of Christian exhortation, telling his listeners it was "your duty to get rich," that worldly success could be a service to God. Life coaches today tend to speak in a psychological rather than spiritual vocabulary. Coaching discourse pursues what the psychologist Abraham Maslow in 1943 called "self-actualization," or "the desire to become more and more what one is."[8] The secret to your success and well-being resides in you already—in your hidden box—and the trick is to access those latent talents and abilities. Rather than acres of diamonds, though, it is contentment that life coaches tend to emphasize, in a pop-psychological language that speaks of self-fulfillment and "core deep issues." But the emphasis remains on working life. The rise of coaching reflects the extent to which Americans are encouraged to identify themselves and their emotional lives with labor; we call them "life" coaches, but they are really "work" coaches, after all.[9]

One of the obvious contradictions in life coaching is the genre's celebration of boldness on the one hand and its actual conformity on the other. You are advised to think outside the box, but of course there is no phrase more inside the box than "outside the box." Leonard tells you to unhook yourself from the future, but worrying about the future is what brings you to a coach in the first place; what's more, many coaches explain the difference between themselves and psychologists by saying that while therapists focus on the past, coaches look to the future. Are you trying to be less anxious and live in the moment? Great, here is a book with *twenty-eight* discrete steps you need to master in order to do this. Coaching is therefore both symptom and cure. Its metaphorical magic hopes to summon something concrete out of a vapor of familiar truisms. And sometimes it works. In one testimonial on the power of coaching, one anguished twenty-four-year-old client, unsure about her professional future, took out a loan to pay a 15,000 dollar fee for a coach to help her find a fulfilling new career. It worked—she became a life coach.[10]

COLLABORATION (N.)
With Bruno Diaz

Collaboration is an idea as old as human endeavor, and like other keywords that seem to lionize partnership and **sharing** it celebrates cooperation, particularly at work. It received the *Harvard Business Review* seal of approval with a 2005 cover story, "Collaboration Rules," which urged managers to nurture work environments that generate "cheap, plentiful interactions" between workers as a way of breaking down organizational barriers and "silos." Its dominant uses therefore relate to but are substantially different from *solidarity*, which remains (so far) unappropriated by corporate jargoneers. Unlike the old-fashioned factory floor or secretarial pool, where colleagues could identify with each other as workers with a common class interest, the new collaborative workplace asks employees to collude with each other as "team members" working to advance the employer's interests.[11]

This way of working has been championed by the consumer-focused research consultancies that have proliferated over the last two decades, which speak an abstract and expensive argot of "**innovation**," "strategy," and "insight." It is an ideal that animates much of the diffuse, and often poorly paid, open-source labor of the web, and it has become an organizing principle of the contemporary workplace, both spatially and intellectually. In many cases, it masks hierarchical discipline behind a veneer of egalitarian voluntarism.

Blue-collar work has long involved "squads" and "gangs," reflecting the *OED*'s primary denotation of collaboration: "united labor, cooperation." Teams, with their clearly delineated roles and sense of play and mutual benefit, have proliferated in a wide variety of workplaces: from the automotive plants where **lean** production got its start to the service industries and white-collar environments where employees are routinely hailed as "team members." Office work has developed a special affection for collaboration, for reasons the *OED* suggests in the rest of its primary definition: it is "united labor," the entry specifies, "especially in literary, artistic, or scientific work." Taking this interpretation as their lead, the last twenty years have seen the kind of consultancies mentioned above rename their departments as "pods," extending the ecological metaphor of the office **ecosystem**; staff appraisals and meetings have been transformed into "catch-ups," "huddles," and "workshops." It's a seductive shift in language, one that has recently leached out of workplaces in the so-called "**creative** industries" to employers once thought of as grey and fuddy-duddy, like investment banks, law firms and the civil service. After all, who wants to go to a stuffy meeting when they could be in a chatty "catch-up," a touchline "huddle," or a literary "workshop"? Who wouldn't prefer to be a dolphin in a "money pod" rather than a pencil-pusher in the "finance department"?

The contrived informality of this vocabulary is meant to tell employees that everyone is in this together, working towards the same meaningful goals. As with a certain ideal of the purpose- and **passion**-driven artist, the work is not driven by the need for a paycheck or the fear of unemployment, but by the worker's own desire for self-actualization. These ideas circulate among both management and labor in the service industries, as a mawkish Target recruitment video addressing prospective store clerks shows with an earnest voiceover that intones, "*you* are what makes *us*." [12] The reorganization of the workforce's nomenclature mirrors a reconfiguration of the office itself. Staff are told to "hotdesk" (a verb) instead of sitting regularly at a single, personal desk. As meetings became "huddles," they were liberated from corporate conference rooms and their chain of command. Instead, they may take place in coffee shops, on rooftops, and even in the park. One London consultancy even has a super-king-size bed right in the office; employees are encouraged to use it for naps and client meetings.

This spatial flattening of professional rank is not wholly new, of course; it builds upon the ideas of transparency and democracy found in the century-old open-plan office. It tells us that the whole workplace, from the wastepaper baskets to the modern art on the walls, is not yours or mine but ours. It is a pastiche of solidarity in which company founders rub shoulders with interns, the receptionist theoretically knows as much about the business as the CEO, and meetings with subordinates are **coaching** sessions. In theory, this repurposing of language and space makes senior management more likely to treat those further down the food chain with understanding and empathy. But collaboration can also mask labor-saving austerity: junior staff must be persuaded that they are important parts of a larger cooperative effort, rather than employees whose time and labor are sold to clients at a huge markup. Encouraged by the collegial use of soft furnishings, they "step up" and take responsibility for work outside their job description and pay grade. It also allows executives the cover of a flattened hierarchy to exploit, bully, and coerce, while the presence of a bed in an office goes some way toward normalizing sexual harassment.

A permanent "last day of school" atmosphere goes beyond the now ubiquitous table football and cornucopia of snack foods. One British consultancy, for example, holds a regular mud-wrestling contest where Lycra-clad employees duke it out in a goo-filled paddling pool while their colleagues look on, cheering and drinking free beer. Beyond the brightly colored walls of the white-collar office, collaboration also masks the danger of redundancy and the low or nonexistent wages of service and internship work. Factory automation, which makes people redundant by replacing them with mechanical substitutes, has been rebranded, with an unintentionally dystopian ring, as "human-robot collaboration." Consultancies have also updated the now commonplace "crowdsourcing," and its suggestion of eager cooperation and even fandom, with "co-creation," to portray the experience and expertise of consultants, clients, and customers as equal partners in the development of brands and products. The commodification of the consumer's labor during this process turns collaboration into a practice not only of production, but also of consumption. "Collaborative consumption," writes one *Forbes* writer, is a method by which "[consumers] get what they need from each other instead of . . . large organizations." Here, "collaboration" is a synonym for sharing that signifies a shift in power from cartels and conglomerates to consumers and **entrepreneurs** via apps and digitized services.[13]

The irony, although none of this is meant to be ironic, is that such collaboration is atomized and hierarchical, not cooperative in any economic sense—that is, it is not shared work in pursuit of shared results. The so-called "teacherpreneurs" of lesson-plan marketplaces like TeachersPayTeachers.com, for instance, sell their lesson plans to other teachers around the country, while the site takes a 15 percent cut—a rentier capture of the routine sharing educators do all the time. It's also an example of how the low pay and exhaustion of one set of workers becomes an exploitable angle—if teachers were paid well, such sites would have little reason to exist. The *OED*'s other definition of collaboration—"cooperation"—once referred to factory work, although this meaning has been lost. This "cooperation" as Marx described it was "the new power that arises from the fusion of many forces into one single force."[14] The sweatshops of the Victorian era (and ours) that cooperated the labor of the proletariat were physically demanding, close and hot, while the collaborative digital workhouses of our own time are diffuse, reliant on intellectual and emotional labor, and comparatively solitary. At least the chairs offer better lumbar support.

COMPETENCY (N.); COMPETENCIES (N. PL.)

When did "competent" go from a synonym for "average" to a *competency*, a superlative term for a skill? And how in the process did the noun acquire its clumsy pluralization? Competencies sounds to the uninitiated like a cumbersome substitute for "skills," just as **curator** is a needlessly grand way to say "someone who owns a store." But as with most of these keywords, competencies carries a deeper, ideological meaning of which its cumbersome pretension is only an initial clue. Like other terms of white-collar work, like "deliverables" and **outcomes**, competencies reduce laboring activity to a set of repeatable, quantifiable tasks. So where did competencies come from? And what did it do with skills?

Obsolete meanings of the count noun "competency" referred to what the *OED* calls "a sufficiency, without superfluity, of the means of life; a competent estate or income." An example of this older usage comes from 1933, when an Iowa lawyer wrote for *Harper's* on the Depression's effects on the small farmers in his state. He observed that "friends and clients of years' standing have lost inherited competencies which had been increased by their own conservative management." This author uses "competency" to describe an estate as modest and unadorned as the Midwestern "pioneer stock" he counts among his clients. The present-day plural, however, doesn't have this modest sense of "sufficiency without superfluity," nor is it an estate or income that can be possessed. Instead, it's a set of qualifications or traits that reside in the person. One example of this sense of competency as character trait comes from its history in schools. Educational competencies were initially benchmarks that students had to pass to move on to the next grade. These were not "skills" (a set of distinctions that belong to the world of work). They were instead "the competencies required for mastery of each phase of each subject," as the *New York Times* reported in October 1963. Over time, "competencies" came to be used for teachers, rather than students, as the term became a quality of labor, rather than of learning. By the 1980s, education researchers wrote about how new technologies in the classroom required teachers "to develop new competencies, to adapt established teaching routines, and to modify the teaching and learning environment." Competencies now belonged to the labor of teachers rather than that of their students, although with the rise of "competency-based education," which assigns course credit for work experience, this usage is shifting back to students. Competency-based education is advertised as "a structure that creates **flexibility**" by allowing students to work at their own pace and in their own place and time, instead of privileging time spent in a classroom. Like many uses of flexibility, this is presented as liberation from noxious regulatory restraints holding people back. For example, the University of Wisconsin (through its flexible option program) and the online Western Governors University (a nonprofit) offer degree programs that grant course credit for work experience. What of education outside of work? The UW program identifies educational competencies as "the skills and knowledge UW faculty *and industry leaders* have identified as essential to your chosen degree or certificate."[15]

On the surface, the divide between skills and competencies looks to be a simple class and professional distinction. The "skilled trades" exist in manufacturing and blue-collar labor, while competencies are a feature of office and managerial work. Yet the words are often used interchangeably, as many consultancy sites and skills (or competency) training curricula show.[16] Given this overlap, there is no shortage of articles devoted to parsing the distinctions. One such effort, from a consultancy called HRSG, begins: "As a competency specialist, we're often asked whether there is any difference between skills and competencies." Naturally, there is a difference, since this company seems to require one as a condition of its existence. The author explains that skills are discrete, while competencies are holistic; so, competencies refer to a broad knowledge base that is inclusive of, but not limited to, skills. Skills tell you what an employee does; competencies assess something more elusive:

> [S]kills don't give us the "how." How does an individual perform a job successfully? How do they behave in the workplace environment to achieve the desired result? Competencies provide that missing piece of the puzzle by translating skills into on-the-job behaviors that demonstrate the ability to perform the job requirements competently.[17]

Competencies therefore belong to the abstract, immaterial world of character, like so many of the words in this book. Other critics, though, are less circumspect about the class distinctions inherent in skills and competencies. According to the website of HRTMS—a firm devoted to "job description management"—"skills are specific learned activities like mopping the floor, using a computer, and stocking merchandise, while competencies are skills + knowledge + behavior like problem solving, communication, or professionalism."[18]

The competency was introduced to business scholarship by C. K. Prahalad and Gary Hamel in a 1990 *Harvard Business Review* article, "The Core Competence of the Corporation." They defined competencies as "the collective learning of the organization." (While the title uses the word "competence" in the singular, Prahalad and Hamel mostly use the plural "competencies" in the article itself). The specter of Japanese ascendancy in manufacturing looms large in the piece, as in so many business concepts that got their start in the 1980s and early 1990s. The authors write that "Western companies" remain bound by "a concept of the corporation that unnecessarily limits the ability of individual businesses to fully exploit the deep reservoir of technological capability," a reference to the complacency in American companies that Japanese firms had avoided. Instead of binding individual employees to a specific task, Prahalad and Hamel argue, Japanese firms exploited the broader "competencies" of their employees, allowing them to bypass hierarchical restrictions in the pursuit of an objective. Prahalad and Hamel's description of the competency leans heavily on aesthetic and psychological language: competencies "harmonize" a firm's know-how and technological capacity; an emphasis on competencies rather than products helps "build a strong feeling of community" among employees; the objective "is communication, involvement, and a deep commitment to working across organizational boundaries." Competency was one example of the broad popularity of management theories that foregrounded employee **collaboration** and **creativity**, rather than discipline and regimentation, as virtues in the workplace.[19]

Another 1980s trend that "core competencies" joined was outsourcing, a circumstance hinted at obliquely in Hamel and Prahalad's article. Nurturing employee loyalty to a competence rather than an organization, they write, should do two things: encourage collaboration within the workplace, and "wean key employees off the idea that they belong in perpetuity to any particular business."[20] A 1994 *Fortune* article on the "tough new downsized world" described competency development as an outsourced employee's only mode of survival. "Very soon, half the work force of the developed world will be outside the organization," the author, Carla Rapaport, wrote. "The future prosperity of all of us will depend on their competencies and their education, yet no one seems to be noticing or caring. If workers don't continually develop and update their skills, not only will they be of no use to the organization but, worse, they will be a growing burden to the rest of us."[21] (Here, Rapaport uses "skills" as well, but her emphasis is on competencies.)

This combination of disciplinary hectoring (don't become a burden to the rest of us by neglecting your competencies) and earnest advice (your prosperity depends on never neglecting your competencies) may sound familiar. This exhausting sense of self-commodification disguised as **freedom** is the beating heart, such as it is, of personal **branding** and the **entrepreneurship** cult. Competencies may be a redundant term, since the value that it supposedly adds—social, intellectual, and emotional traits—could just as easily be described as "skills." But skills are a classed term, without the prestige of the competency. And while skills may be required for a job, skills like carpentry, cooking, welding, arithmetic, or writing are portable—that is, you get to take them home. They belong to you; core competencies, however, belong to your boss.

CONVERSATION (N.)

Conversation has become a widespread term for any large-scale, mass-mediated social interchange. We have national conversations about hot-button issues, like racial segregation or economic inequality; angry political activists are regularly invited by their antagonists to join a demobilizing "dialogue"; and news media routinely invite their readers, listeners, and viewers to "join the conversation" by sending a tweet or letter to the editor. Indeed, the more remote the possibility or improbable the productivity of a face-to-face chat about an issue becomes, the more likely it is that the public treatment of that issue will be described as a "conversation."

Mass media across the US ideological spectrum employ the euphemism of the conversation to refer to any managed interaction with their consumers, in a letters page or via social media and online comment threads. A literal conversation—as when you talk to another human—is ideally collegial, friendly, and direct, unmediated by social rank or medium. It takes place between peers, at arm's reach. Taken literally, therefore, a conversation has very little in common with any individual's actual relationship to any bureaucratic institution, much less the modern mass media and advertising industries. And this is partly the point: the metaphorical conversation allows private and public mass media to negotiate their audience's fragmentation as well as their skepticism. As a marketing term, the conversation seeks explicitly to counter people's alienation from advertising by pretending it isn't advertising. In Joseph Jaffe's *Join the Conversation: How to Engage Marketing-Weary Consumers with the Power of Community, Dialogue, and Partnership*, "conversation" is a synonym for "marketing," but a particular variety of marketing in which the consumer is doing much of the work for free.[22]

In the political sphere, the model of the conversation is also the preferred rhetorical device by which social conflicts are routed into the therapeutic form of a dialogue. In a nominally democratic culture like the United States, in which dissent is tolerated up to the point it seeks to disrupt the institutions it targets, political opposition is routinely framed as an opportunity for dialogue. In a dialogue, all participants are on the same side, troubled by shared problems, pursuing a common **outcome**. In the United States, the most influential political use of the conversation motif is the "national conversation about race," a phrase popularized by Bill Clinton's 1997 "Initiative on Race," a White House project chaired by the scholar John Hope Franklin.[23] In town-hall-style speaking events that he chaired as part of the Initiative, Clinton repeatedly invoked a talking cure model of racial reconciliation, regularly instructing participants to be blunt. The "national conversation on race" returned to heavy circulation with Barack Obama's election, and Michael P. Jeffries dates its renewed popularity even more precisely—to Obama's famous 2008 "More Perfect Union" speech in Philadelphia, when the candidate spoke personally and introspectively, and thus conversationally, about race and religion.[24] In spite of the encouragement of bluntness and honesty, the "national conversation on race" is a rhetorical means by which racism is loudly *avoided* in US media and politics. Since a "national conversation" about anything is a logical impossibility, many if not most uses of the phrase in print are actually about how the conversation never did, never will, or never should take place.[25] National conversations are distinguished by what they avoid saying, rather than for what they actually do say. A "conversation about race," for example, is a way to signal one's good-faith seriousness on racial questions without saying the word "racism." Indeed, the fact that such a deep social and political cleavage is treated as the subject of a conversation at all is evidence of how unseriously it is taken. The National League Central or last night's *Jeopardy* are good subjects for a conversation; for racism, we're going to need a bigger boat.

CONTENT (N.)

In a 2014 press release announcing its acquisition of the much-loved TV comedy *South Park* and a yet-to-be-loved comedy, *The Hotwives of Orlando,* the streaming service Hulu trumpeted its

expanding "library of exclusive, current and library content."
Hulu's senior vice president and head of content Craig Erwich
wrote:

> I could not be more thrilled to announce that we are contin-
> uing the momentum this year by bringing new seasons of our
> beloved Originals, as well as the premiere of our brand new
> title "The Hotwives of Orlando" and new library deals that
> will make Hulu's content offering more **robust** and diverse
> than ever before.[26]

In volume 1 of *Capital,* Marx famously explained commodity
fetishism under capitalism as an alienating social world in which,
for workers,

> the social relations between their private labors appear as what
> they are, i.e. they do not appear as direct social relations be-
> tween persons in their work, but rather as material relations
> between persons and social relations between things.[27]

The reversal contained in Marx's phrase—manufactured things
take on the dynamic richness of people, while people themselves
are reduced to objects—is what bothers many critics of the proliferation of the term "content" in the contemporary culture industries. One form of this criticism objects to the degradation of
art ("quality content") by its confusion with fluff.[28] But *Breaking Bad* and *Moby Dick* are commodities, of course, insofar as
they are sold to advertisers, viewers, or readers in exchange for
money. The problem with content runs deeper than the boundary between high art and low culture, to the privatization of the
desires, knowledge, and experiences we gain from the stories we
read, watch, and remember. Content names artistic and narrative
creativity, and therefore creators themselves, as things like any
other.

   "Content" is ubiquitous in print and digital media—television, film, and music producers in particular use the term regularly, while book publishers and journalists, perhaps protective
of the antiquity and prestige of their media, are less fond of the
word and often invoke it with derision. The rise of content in

its current form can be traced to the high-speed web. In 2000, *Time* reported the merger of AOL and Time Warner by explaining that the new technology of "broadband" originates in "the fat, fast pipes of cable television that could carry vast amounts of Internet content." The anachronistic materiality of this description, which now seems silly—the internet as a series of fat pipes—points out how "content" once underscored what was then the novel, disorienting immateriality of literary and visual media trafficked through the web. This is not to wring hands about the rise of ebooks and small screens and the decline of print and cinema but rather to emphasize how digitization is an intensification of the commodification of all forms of culture, rather than a departure from it.[29]

The *Corpus of Historical American English* shows that pre-2000 uses of the word "content" mostly followed the *OED*'s strict definition, and its print bias: "the things contained or treated in a writing or document; the various subdivisions of its subject matter," or what is found in a book's table of contents. Content was the material *in* a book or on a television network, not the book or television program itself. The term also thrived in the 1990s in calls for government regulation of music, movies, and video games. Tipper Gore often repeated an anecdote about her harrowing 1985 encounter with Prince's "Darling Nikki" that motivated her to launch a crusade against "graphic content" in popular culture. In phrases like "violent content," "sexual content," or, the fruit of Gore's labors, the "explicit content" of the parental advisory stickers affixed to CD covers, the word refers to knowledge and information that should be policed. In this context, content is a purposely bland euphemism for any controversial narrative, visual, or verbal elements of a work of art. Gore understood content as the evidence by which an artistic work could be judged and condemned without any attempt at interpretation beyond literal denotation. This anticipates the contemporary ubiquity of the term to describe everything transmitted through the fat tubes of the internet. Today, content is just an immaterial substance made of digital words, which is how

Merriam-Webster's pleasingly cheeky definition now describes it: "the principal substance (as written matter, illustrations, or music) offered by a World Wide Web site."[30]

Much of this digital substance is harvested on so-called content farms, websites that cheaply and quickly produce articles meant to optimize search results. Outfits like eHow.com and the defunct Associated Content have used low-paid writers to produce articles intended to game Google results and thereby build a stockpile of "content" used to sell targeted ads. Content-substance is undistinguished either generically, by subject matter, by level of specialization, or by style. It is a marketer's term, used to describe anything that generates views, subscriptions, or ticket sales.[31] "Content" in education, meanwhile, refers to everything that is contained in a curriculum. California's Common Core standards informational sheet, for example, refers throughout to "content areas"—what one might otherwise call a "discipline" or a "subject," like history or math.[32] Content is any quantifiable artistic or intellectual substance that can be measured, repeated, and reliably delivered, at the lowest cost to the owners of capital.

CREATIVE (ADJ., N.); CREATIVITY (N.)

Creative and its variants are a versatile part of the vocabulary of contemporary capitalism, able to link imagination, aesthetic practice, and religious faith in the pursuit of private gain. The oldest word on creativity's family tree is "creation," whose first meaning was specifically Christian—the term for the divine genesis of the universe. One of the newest is the nominal form of creative, normally an adjective for an original thinker or idea. Creative is now also a count noun (think of the creatives who may be moving into your shrinking rust-belt city) and a mass noun (get creative on the horn, said account services to production). Many people would probably agree that creativity is an essential human trait and crucial to a happy life, though this noun is a relatively new coinage. An even more recent development is the notion that creativity is a trait of capitalist markets. And in the United States, the political phrase "job creators" borrows some of creation's residual divine light to illuminate the benevolent fiat of the capitalist, who is thought to create jobs out of the formless void.

If creation has been divine, creativity is decidedly human. The most important conflict in the etymological history of "creative" is the struggle between its religious and secular meanings. Before the late nineteenth century, to the degree that people could participate in something called "creation," it was only to approximate the purity of the original, capital-C Creation, rather than inaugurating their own. "There is nothing new under the sun," Ecclesiastes reminded humans inclined to creative hubris. "The created cannot create," (*creatura no potest creare*) added St. Augustine, insisting that such power resided only in God, and not in his creations.[33] In the history of the word "creative," there are actually two decisive rifts: this initial one between the divine and the human creation suggested here, and then, once creativity became a human trait, a division between its aesthetic and productive forms.[34] We can roughly date this latter conflict to around 1875, the earliest example of the word "creativity" given in the *OED*, from an essay on Shakespeare's singular brilliance.[35] Creativity was a work of imagination rather than production, of artistry rather than labor. One of the consequences of this split between art and work has been to valorize creativity as the domain of an intuitive, singular, historically male genius. Productive creativity, meanwhile, is not art but labor, and thus rarely earns the title of creativity at all; this is the supposedly unimaginative labor of the manual worker or the farmer and the often feminized work of social reproduction.[36] There are obvious class and gender prejudices at work here; coaxing a crop out of stubborn soil or preparing a family meal with limited ingredients are not typically seen as creative acts, whereas cooking a restaurant meal with the harvested crops often is. Other differences are rather arbitrary. Children's play is not thought to be brilliant in the way Shakespeare is; it may, however, qualify as creative because it appears (to adults, anyway) to be intuitive.

The widespread popularity of creative in economic discourse today suggests that this old breach between the imaginative and the productive has partly been closed. The idiosyncratic, eccentric, even oppositional posture of the creative artist is now an economic asset, chased by real-estate developers and promoted by self-help writers as comparable to the spirit of the **entrepreneur**.[37] The popularity of "creativity" as an economic value in English can be traced to two major sources—Joseph Schumpeter, twentieth-century economist and theorist of "creative destruction," and Richard Florida, the University of Toronto scholar whose book, *The Rise of the Creative Class*, became one of the most celebrated and influential urban policy texts of the early 2000s. "The bourgeoisie cannot exist without constantly revolutionizing the instruments of production, and thereby the relations of production, and with them the whole relations of society," wrote Marx and Engels in the *Manifesto of the Communist Party*. In his 1942 classic *Capitalism, Socialism, and Democracy*, Schumpeter agreed, up to a point. As we saw in the chapter on entrepreneurs, Schumpeter shared Marx's sense of capitalism as a destructive and also transformative historical process, but he reframed Marx's history of class struggle motivated by exploitation as an evolutionary process driven by visionary entrepreneurs. By opening new markets and breaking down old industrial processes, Schumpeter wrote, capitalism "incessantly revolutionizes the economic structure *from within,* incessantly destroying the old one, incessantly creating a new one." This process is what Schumpeter called "creative destruction."[38]

"Creative" here refers to the work of forging new modes of production, new **markets**, and new products, but it also had a touch of artistry: the ingenuity, vision, and intuition to make things anew. Even so, creativity still belonged more to the artists' studio than the corner office until the last half of the twentieth century in the United States, when it came to describe a productive aspect of the psychology of individual workers. Sarah Brouillette has shown how much the familiar accoutrements of today's progressive office culture—foosball tables, bright colors, and other perks ostensibly meant to cultivate employees' creativity and loyalty—owe to the psychologist Abraham Maslow, famous for his 1943 theory of a "hierarchy of human needs." Maslow, Brouillette writes, "began imagining all business culture as an outlet for and source of work- ers' enterprising individual self-fulfillment." Florida's notion of "artistic creativity," which he regards as integrated with other va- rieties (economic and technological) is based on the presumption that "art" equals "self-expression," a historically specific assump- tion which, like "creativity" itself, is mistaken for a universal and timeless idea. Indeed, it is this particularly modernist understand- ing of artistic work as solitary and idiosyncratic, oriented towards the expression of the artist's unique self, that also came to suit US geopolitical interests in the Cold War, as many scholars of US and Latin American modernism have shown. Rob Pope, in his his- tory of creativity, includes two other examples of creativity's Cold War deployments. The US psychologist Carl Rogers argued that a prosperous nation like the United States needed "freely creative original thinkers," not ladder-climbing conformists. If the grey Soviet system encouraged the latter, the multi-colored capitalism of the United States required creative free thinkers. It is this per- ceived cultural strength, not just newer and better weapons, that will beat Communism, J. P. Guilford argued in 1959.[39]

Florida believes strongly in the naturalness and timelessness of this relatively new idea, creativity; he describes it as "what sets us apart from all other species." Florida elevates creative capi- talists from a social type, which they remain in Schumpeter's theory of the entrepreneur, to a social class, one that Florida estimates as constituting a third of the American working pop- ulation. Its members include scientists and engineers, architects and artists, musicians and teachers—anyone, in short, "whose economic function is to create new ideas, new technology, and new creative **content**." The creative class shares certain tastes and preferences, like nonconformity, an appreciation for merit, a desire for social diversity, and an appetite for "serendipity," the chance encounter facilitated by urban life. A taste for city life, in fact, is one of the creative class's most treasured preferences, and

Florida's ideas promised to leverage these to repopulate declining urban centers without significant public expenditure on social welfare or infrastructure. Politicians in various postindustrial cities in the Global North became eager customers of the consultancy spawned by the success of *The Rise of the Creative Class*. We will find in Florida's account scarcely a trace of the breach that Williams described between imaginative and productive creativity. Creativity, Florida writes, is the "font from which new technologies, new industries, new wealth, and all other good economic things flow." Art, music, and social diversity are no longer independent values, but rather values dependent on their appeal to high-wage knowledge workers.[40]

Why creativity now? Jamie Peck, one of Florida's most unsparing critics, argues that beginning in the 1970s, deindustrializing cities were faced with a dearth of available economic development options. They began competing with one another not only for increasingly mobile jobs, but for places in a consumer economy in which cities became commodities themselves. Abandoning comprehensive urban planning, city governments focused instead on what Peck calls "urban fragments" with potential in this consumer market—single districts with marketable appeal due to their theaters or arenas, historic architecture, proximity to job-rich downtowns, or some other marketable feature. (Often, these urban fragments become the sort of generic, purpose-built developments the suburban-born creatives were supposedly fleeing, like the new creative-class Potemkin village north of downtown Detroit with the odd name The District Detroit, an ode to urbanity that only a marketer could love, or even understand.) The creative city becomes a place where a mobile middle class can participate in this consumer economy as workers and residents. Since there is a broad affinity between one's economic and imaginative activity in the Floridian regime of creativity, you "live, work, and play," in the familiar liturgy of bourgeois urban life, as an economic subject at all hours. Even artistic activity that might have once appeared oppositional or radical—Florida claims to be a big fan of rap music—merely buttresses the "creative index" of the city (a metric he developed).

"Whereas classical liberal *doxa* assumes that what we are and what we own must not be confused," writes Brouillette, neoliberals favor a "union of economic rationality and authenticity, this perfect marriage between the bohemian and what had been her bourgeois other." The extra-economic values of the artist and the priorities of the market are no longer treated as autonomous, much less antagonistic, but harmonious. As Brouillette emphasizes, however, it would be a mistake to read the rise of the creative class as a colonization of the once-pure realms of the artistic imagination by the market.[41] The rise of the so-called creative class is not a heroes-and-villains plot of businessmen corrupting creativity. This would be far too flattering to artists and writers, who are hardly innocent bystanders. Rather, the business world has valorized unexamined ideas of what "artistry" means and turned an individualistic, class-bound idea of "the artist" toward **market** goals. These meanings of artistry have evolved over the years in complex ways, but the one that circulates in the economic use of creativity dates to the origins of the word "creativity" in the late nineteenth century. Then, as Gustavus Stadler has shown, creativity was closely aligned with nineteenth-century ideas of "genius" and "inspiration," which were seen as the fruit of an "irreducible originality," rather than a social process.[42] As the cult of the entrepreneur shows, this fantasy of irreducible originality is still with us. Sometimes, there really is nothing new under the sun.

CURATOR (N.); CURATE (V.)

Judas Priest doesn't just release a greatest-hits album, Metallica and Slipknot *curate* it. A high-end sneaker store doesn't sell shoes, it *curates* them. Web-based media are "**content** curators." An event planner in New Zealand will not simply plan your organization's next fundraiser but will rather "curate an experience" for clients. And in today's fast-paced world, how can "high-net-worth individuals" find the time to "interact with luxury **brands**" without a curator? You probably didn't even think to dignify throwing out your moth-eaten sweaters as curatorial work. But as one frantic closet cleaner writes on a fashion blog:

> With the death of average in mind, we must cull from our wardrobe removing from it all that looks average. We must become our own curators. Becoming a curator, however, not only takes effort, it takes practice. If you're anything like so many of my friends, then your wardrobe is overflowing with goods. For them, cutting it back, curating it to include only the exceptional, is not only a daunting task, it's a paralyzing one.

Curators have proliferated in the media and commercial worlds, according to one account, as a form of pretension by which relatively humble pursuits like shoe-selling attain the lofty heights of the trained connoisseur.[43] In this way, something we might have once called "selecting" or "editing" is treated as a form of expertise equivalent to the work of a museum scholar. And there's plenty of truth to this, but a simply eye-rolling response to the term's puffed-up overreach overlooks a deeper economic logic at work, one inflected by the rise of a low-wage, precarious service economy and its gendered division of labor.

Curating's migration from the academy to the boutique is about claiming for the latter the prestige of the former, but it's also about substituting prestige for more tangible forms of compensation. It also brings the caring function that is at the etymological root of the curator and the curate (the former associated with museums and the latter with churches) into the service sector. This is significant, since the verb "to curate" belongs to sectors like fashion retail, associated with female labor. The rallying cry of university unions, "We Can't Eat Prestige," was coined by the female white-collar support staff at Harvard in the mid-1970s, an example of how care workers are meant to substitute moral or emotional incentives—prestige, a feeling of pride in "doing good"—for financial rewards.[44]

This connection to care work comes from the word's etymology. Before it became associated with the work of museum academics, curation had a mostly religious meaning. In the Catholic and Anglican Churches, a curate is a priest at the local level entrusted with the care (Latin *cura*) of souls. The verb "curate" is a back-formation of the noun, derived from the Latin *curare*, "to care for," and *curator*, a "guardian" or, tellingly, "overseer." There is something of both in the contemporary consumer-capitalist curator. On the one hand, selling sneakers becomes a work of aesthetic expertise and spiritual comfort. On the other, my experience of selection is no longer entirely my own—it is handled for me by Spotify playlist generators and e-commerce algorithms. A fitting credo for online **entrepreneurs**, according to *Forbes* magazine, is "curate and control."[45] The curator's combination of moral purpose, control, and **creativity** aligns him closely with the **innovator** and the entrepreneur. In the most enthusiastic celebrations of each, marketing ingenuity and aesthetic imagination are scarcely distinguishable from one another. The rise of the retail curator captures this commodification of creativity by combining in a rhetorical flourish the function of the manager and that of the artist or caretaker. Curators have always been both "bureaucrat and priest," as the art critic David Levi Strauss writes.[46] The contemporary spread of the curator, therefore, is novel only in its expansion of the priestly side of this equation to the care, not of souls, but of wardrobes and palates. Yet most curators at sneaker stores, of course, just work there, for wages supplemented by whatever prestige they can scrape up.

Like entrepreneurship and innovation, curating as a business practice presents profit-seeking activities as the pursuit of truth and beauty. It also captures some myths about Big **Data** and the democratic spirit of the Internet. Shopping curators exist to cull the variety of goods online. Online publishing democratizes information access and authorship itself, as one author in *The Guardian*'s business section gushes in a profile of the "new breed of media businesses that see themselves more as curators of content rather than owners."[47] Such business journalists guilelessly presume that the way media moguls "see themselves" is in fact the way they are: all priest, no bureaucrat.

DATA (N.)

Data, the beloved android officer on the Starship Enterprise in *Star Trek: The Next Generation*, is so named because he is a superhuman consolidator and analyst of information in computerized form. Since he is a character defined by his unmet desire for an emotional life, he is also a sympathetic character to all human viewers who recognize in him their own befuddlement in the face of their own feelings. But because he lacks subjective feelings about the information encoded in his neural net, the kindly Data represents a technological fantasy about artificial intelligence and, indeed, data itself: that it is a **smart,** unprejudiced, and politically neutral sorter of information, which desires to emulate the human without dominating it. Lt. Commander Data and the myth of data aspire to cooperation, not power.

Data in its common usage is the plural of the rarely heard count-noun "datum," defined as "related items of information considered collectively": it is also "the quantities, characters, or symbols on which operations are performed by a computer and which may be stored or transmitted in the form of electrical signals and held on recording media"; it is, more succinctly, "information represented in digital form." Data is also a commodity, especially in the era of widespread consumer use of the internet. Metadata—data that organizes other data, like user names and traits—is generated by everything users do on sites like Facebook, Amazon, Gmail, and through other applications on their smartphones. Facebook, Amazon, Google/Alphabet, Apple, Microsoft, and other private corporations use the data they generate for purposes that are often opaque, secretive, and, of course, under their proprietary control. The dream of data, and Data, is the apparent neutrality of each; data, however, is shaped by the prejudices and interests of the institutions and researchers who generate it, by the algorithms they write, and by the questions they ask—or don't. As the Borg Queen tells Data when her pitiless intergalactic cyborg empire captures him in *Star Trek: First Contact*: "You are an imperfect being, created by an imperfect being. Finding your weakness is only a matter of time."

Because data is ostensibly neutral and the technological applications that create and manage it are so complicated to a layperson, the politics of its use can be obscure. This is especially true of "Big Data," an ambiguous and often capitalized term that sometimes sounds like a skeptical term for monopoly power (like Big Oil or Big Pharma); a technological condition (the actual scale of information generated by networked computers); a strategy of managing that condition to "unlock its value"; and, in some cases, a utopian horizon of information management, "humanity's dashboard," as one enthusiast, Steve Lohr, optimistically described it. Big Data, purred the *New York Times* in 2011, will do nothing less than "for the first time reveal sociological laws of human behavior," thereby enabling policy makers "to predict political crises, revolutions and other forms of social and economic instability, just as physicists and chemists can predict natural phenomena."[1]

A 2001 report by Doug Laney did not use the term Big Data, but it is widely credited with first articulating the problem of digital information management that the term addresses. "E-commerce," Laney wrote, "has exploded data management challenges along three dimensions: volumes, velocity, and variety." So Big Data, in this case, describes the size of data sets, the speed with which they must be analyzed and shared with users, and the enormous variety of information generated on the web: think of everything you have searched, read, liked, or written on a screen in the past week, and multiply it by the number of smartphone users around the world.

Then think about who might own and control this data. Against the transparency and utilitarian efficiency promised by the ideal of Big Data as "humanity's dashboard" is Frank Pasquale's metaphor of the "Black Box," the privately owned, secret recorder of our digital data transfers and identities, which he explores in a recent book on data surveillance and digital technologies. Given the fact that much of the world's digital data is controlled by five secretive firms, the Black Box metaphor emphasizes the secrecy and surveillance that is the bread and butter of corporate data management, especially in Silicon Valley. "To scrutinize others while avoiding scrutiny oneself is one of the most important forms of power," Pasquale writes.[2] The Borg Queen would surely agree.

DESIGN (N.)

Design is a word with two common meanings and a third, conspiratorial sense having become mostly pluralized as "designs." The first, "a plan conceived in the mind," captures some of the idiosyncrasy and imagination of **creativity**, and the second, "a preliminary drawing or sketch; a plan, outline, or model" is the more realized, practical work of a designer, the one who brings these foggy conceptions to life. In management consulting and the computing industries, where "design thinking" is quite popular, the word is used in both of these senses.

Design thinking has spread widely from its origins in commercial product design at the Palo Alto firm IDEO, famous for designing the Apple mouse and well known recently for its work in organizational and systems design. Design thinking has become influential in nonprofits, social services, and humanitarian relief. It is taught at a number of universities, where its development as a management philosophy has occasioned the migration of design from the engineering school to the business school. Most definitions of design thinking emphasize empathy and optimism—empathy for the user of a product and optimism about the utility of that product and the design process generally—to solve difficult organizational problems. IDEO's Tim Brown and Jocelyn Wyatt define it this way:

> Design thinking incorporates constituent or consumer insights in depth and rapid prototyping, all aimed at getting beyond the assumptions that block effective solutions. Design thinking—inherently optimistic, constructive, and experiential—addresses the needs of the people who will consume a product or service and the infrastructure that enables it.[3]

Stanford University's Hasso Plattner Institute of Design, better known as the d.school, offers an online introduction to "design thinking" that describes its most important feature as "empathy." IDEO echoes that sentiment by arguing that "design thinking encourages organizations to focus on the people they're creating for and leads to human-centered products, services, and internal processes." The sentimental rhetoric of design thinking helps make its methods portable—it can be found in primary schools, private corporations, and nonprofits, promising to bring "human-centered" empathy to all manner of for-profit corporations, schools, and even prisons (even private ones!). This rhetoric also makes it hard to understand what exactly design thinking *is*. The d.school opens their "About Us" page by declaring, "The d.school helps people develop their creative abilities. It's a place, a community, and a mindset," and to judge from the rest of the school's marketing materials, it's not a mindset that overvalues clarity.[4] Design thinking, scholar Lilly Irani writes, "stands for a critique of rationalistic, impersonal, and quantitative forms of corporate knowing." She argues that it emerged in Northern California in the mid-2000s as a response to outsourcing. At IDEO, an early focus on product design gave way to systems and organizational design—management consulting, in other words—as the firm faced increased competition from Chinese firms. As Irani writes, IDEO retrenched around the ostensibly un-outsourcable skills of empathy, care, and creativity, marking what one of the firm's machinists described to her as a turn from the "mechanical" to the "mystical." The technical, mechanical, "left-brained" skills of product design—programming and grinding—could be ceded to Asia; the "right-brained" skills of empathy and creativity were to remain in California. Design thinking, in Irani's account, thus presumes a kind of Asiatic mode of production for the twenty-first century, in which racialized forms of impersonal labor and quantitative knowledge are outsourced abroad, while empathetic work and qualitative knowledge remain a specialty of first-world creative-class workers.[5]

The language of **innovation** is often spoken in a tone that betrays a paradoxical combination of grandiose evangelism and task-oriented practicality, an impersonal celebration of technology, and an earnest celebration of aesthetic idiosyncrasies. In places like the *Harvard Business Review,* Inc.com, in much of the mainstream media, and in many foundation mission statements, one encounters a similar rhetoric of design that is suspicious of utopian political solutions to social problems—if the possibility is acknowledged at all—but optimistically ambitious in its appraisal of potential technical solutions. As fewer and fewer billionaires consolidate the world's wealth, search and you shall find endless listicles promising "eight innovations to end world hunger." Cholera has scarcely ever had it so good, but we are living in a golden age of toilet design. Competitions for inventive, cheaply-built commodes designed for use in third-world mega-slums or remote villages without modern sanitation are common occurrences; **solutions** like the Caltech toilet or the Ecological Urinal have made headlines.[6] The problem here is not that there are clever engineers who take sanitation and toilet design seriously; rather, it is that in design thinking these solutions are unmoored from a political program that might address the inequities that make them necessary in the first place. This is a perspective encouraged by imagining resource problems as design problems. It's a perspective that depoliticizes scarcity, treating it as a technical problem rather than one of resource inequality or exploitation.

It is easy to see the appeal of imagining world hunger or cholera simply as technical puzzles responsive to human ingenuity. It's optimistic, and it allows us some semblance of the old modernist dream of technological solutions to scarcity in the absence of the political and social programs (whether in their Soviet, third-worldist, or liberal forms) that once sustained those dreams. Design thinking is generally uncritical of **market**-based solutions to systems design problems, as IDEO's work with a for-profit network of secondary schools in Peru makes clear. It stakes a claim on democracy, meanwhile, through its study and celebration of the user or consumer. Again, though, in the absence of a political critique of the structural circumstances constraining a user's **choices**, that optimism can sound more like wishful thinking. One influential book on design thinking for public education reform urges teachers to adopt an "abundance mentality," stressing the importance of an optimistic worldview. "Like all modern managerial philosophies that stake their names in innovation," Megan Erickson writes of its use in public education, design thinking offers "magic, the only alchemy that matters."[7]

DISRUPTION (N.)

Disruption is one of the most widely used and most widely disparaged terms in this book. Its celebration of rebellion and novelty has made it a **brand** identity for all manner of products. Uber disrupts taxicabs; the iPhone disrupts the cell-phone industry; Stance, an upscale hosier favored by Justin Trudeau and Jay-Z, disrupts socks. Universities, reliably late arrivals to the trend, disrupt themselves with "flipped" classrooms and other labor-saving technologies. In these cases, the verb is used positively, as a synonym of "reinvent" or "move forward." In politics, meanwhile, an older, more negative political meaning of "disruption" still applies, denied the laurels heaped upon its technological connotation. When college students "disrupt" right-wing speakers on their campus, they earn widespread media scorn for it. When an activist group named #DisruptJ20 aimed, as the *OED* defines the word, to "break or burst asunder" the inauguration festivities of the forty-fifth president, protesters were subjected to mass trials for conspiracy to riot. Among the general public and in the more thoughtful corners of the business press, overuse has made disruption a target of weary scorn.[8] Critics associate corporate "disruption" with its synonym, "destruction," and with corporate villains like Martin Shkreli, the pharmaceutical profiteer, or Peter Thiel, the thin-skinned venture capitalist. One case in point is the widely mocked startup Bodega, named after the New York City corner stores whose business model it promised to burst asunder with a computer-automated pantry to be installed in upscale apartment lobbies. Audaciously taking its name from the shops it set out to displace and superfluous if not sinister in the actual service it purported to offer—a sort of glorified vending machine with facial recognition software— Bodega crystallized the venality of the tech economy. All that technical expertise, and for what?

The oldest usages for "disrupt" describe a political, economic, or military threat to an established position. Many nineteenth-century uses of the word, for example, referred to the American secession crisis and the Civil War.[9] The positive reclamation of forceful rending as social progress is the major change in disruption's fortunes. And for this, we have the Harvard Business School professor Clayton Christensen mostly to thank. In his 1997 bestseller *The Innovator's Dilemma*, he coined the term "disruptive **innovation**," which he defines against what he calls "sustaining innovation," the improvements and tweaks a firm makes to its already successful product line. Satisfying its existing customers can paradoxically leave a successful firm vulnerable to "disruptive" newcomers; this is the "innovator's dilemma" of his title. In the follow-up book *The Innovator's Solution* (co-authored with Michael Raynor), Christensen and Raynor explain that disruptive innovations take two forms. They can be "low-end" disruptions—cheaper, simpler versions of existing products that are unprofitable for the incumbent manufacturer to pursue.

Or they can be "new-market" disruptions, a competing new product or service that a committed incumbent is unwilling or unable to address, opening the field to a "first mover." While the sustaining innovator gives the customer what he wants, the "disruptive innovator" gives the customer what he does not yet know he needs—or, in the case of a low-end disruption, *only* that which he needs, and nothing more, but at a lower price.[10]

Other business theorists have pondered the question of what motivates or inhibits large-scale manufacturers in the pursuit of new ideas and products, but Christensen's decision to call it "disruption" must be one of the great academic branding exercises of all time.[11] "Disruption" adds a dangerous, rebellious élan to what is, in Christensen's major case study, the otherwise dry combat of disk-drive manufacturers in the early 1980s. The concept has come under scrutiny as its popularity has soared, however. The business historians Andrew A. King and Baljir Baatartogtokh challenged the theory's empirical foundations by surveying scholars and executives in various industries cited as case studies in Christensen's work. Their analysis finds that Christensen and Raynor overemphasize the importance of executive decisions and oversimplify historical context to suit an overarching explanation for economic causality. In *The Innovator's Solution*, nineteenth-century urban stockyards are cited as a historical example of an industry vulnerable to "disruption" by refrigerated railcars. King and Baatartogtokh argue that more credit for the demise of small-scale slaughter operations belongs to the Union Army's demand for beef and the economies of scale offered by "disassembly" plants in cities like Chicago. The Civil War, in other words, did more than any "first mover" could to disrupt craft butchery.[12]

Whatever its empirical advantages or failings, it is as a capitalist morality tale that the drama of disruption finds the greatest influence. As Jill Lepore argued about *The Innovator's Dilemma*, disruption has a distinct missionary tenor. If innovation is our technocratic substitute for the nineteenth-century idea of progress, then disruption offers "the hope of salvation against the very damnation it describes," Lepore writes. "Disrupt, and you will be saved."[13] Christensen's faith in the power of up-starts to unseat incumbents has a populist appeal suited to an era whose "men of progress" are often software developers defined by idiosyncrasies like dropping out of Harvard or a fondness for hooded sweatshirts. Disruption's moral appeal is apparent, as well, in the language of epic and combat that its advocates employ. Borrowing Joseph Schumpeter's fondness for nautical metaphors—"the perennial gale of **creative** destruction" is a frequently quoted example—Christensen and Raynor in *The Innovator's Solution* imagine the executive as a mariner studying the winds and currents.[14] They explain what causes well-run companies to "get killed": once they get a "foothold," disrup-tors will "ultimately crush the incumbents." Elsewhere, one can find business seminars advertising elite American soldiers as experts in "disruption."[15] Running a business is imagined as exploration and warfare, rather than a fairly comfortable pro-fessional existence that generally rewards avoiding unnecessary risks. In this way, even the managerial class is pressured by the relentless economization of life that is a defining feature of our era of austerity for most workers: the constant worry, the sense that work is never ceasing, that an opportunity is perpetually slipping away.

Despite this sense of dread and anxiety, as Lepore insists, dis-ruption cannot be understood apart from its sunnier cousin, in-novation. Where innovation is a theory of rebirth, we can think of disruption as an eschatology: an economic theology of the end of things, whether a local bodega, an incumbent corporation, or a public school district. As a business eschatology, disruption is well suited to a period of economic instability. The financial crisis of 2008 was a "disruption" of the financial markets, as many called it, using the conventionally negative meaning of the word.[16] Disruptions of financial markets yield disaster; but this particular disruption was caused by the disruptive innovation of mortgage-backed securities, which muddles things a bit. Most theories of disruption implicitly seem to accept at some level a basic principle of Marxist economics, that capitalism is prone to destructive crisis. The disruptive innovator does not see this as a weakness, however, but rather as an asset and a source of advantage. "This is an era of disruption," declares an author in the *Harvard Business Review,* surely not intending to sound as dismal and dreadful as he does. "Not disruption as the occasional event, but disruption as the constant, chronic condition of our professional lives."[17]

DIY [DO-IT-YOURSELF] (ADJ.)

In a 2014 column in the *New York Times,* architecture critic Jayne Merkel argued that the underfunded New York City Housing Authority could address its vast backlog of unfinished repairs by training residents to make their own repairs. She called this "A DIY fix for public housing." Like related terms **maker** and **artisanal**, DIY, or do-it-yourself, has a long history, but it is experiencing a revival in its newest iteration as a term of twenty-first century austerity individualism. In Merkel's usage, DIY celebrates individual derring-do in the face of structural forces, such as New York City housing prices and federal disinvestment from public housing.

DIY has had two major associations, which in different ways contribute to its current popularity and politics: these are DIY as amateur home repair and as countercultural practice. The rise of "do-it-yourself" as a description of home repair dates to the middle of the twentieth century. By 1950, the classified section of *Popular Mechanics* advertised an array of tools and tutorials to do-it-yourselfers. More Americans lived in owner-occupied homes than ever before—thirty million by 1960, ten times the number in 1890—and a majority now worked for wages paid by someone else outside the home. The growth of home ownership and the increasingly common spatial separation of home and work created the conditions for "doing it yourself" as a middle-class, mostly male pursuit. "When industrialization separated living and working spaces," Steven Gelber writes, "it also separated

men and women into non-overlapping spheres of competence."
But the desire to do-it-yourself came not just from economic necessity, argues Gelber. It was a satisfying hobby for desk-bound
workers and a respectable way for men to share the labor of the
home while asserting a degree of autonomy and expertise within
it. Even as the exclusively male claim on "do-it-yourself" culture
has frayed, any Home Depot commercial or *Home Improvement*
rerun will remind us of the anxious performance of masculinity
that comes with basic home repair.[18]

The countercultural meaning of DIY (here, most often as an
acronym) is often dated to the short-lived 1976-77 London punk
zine *Sniffin' Glue*. It popularized a DIY aesthetic, a graphic language built on xeroxed pages and handwritten or cut-and-pasted
type, and a writing style celebrating the intimate subcultures of
bands and artists. This ethos and style drew on older sources—
from the 1960s Whole Earth catalog in the United States, instrumental in the rise of maker culture, to the supporters' fanzines
long popular among English soccer fans.[19] If DIY is no longer a
male preserve in home repair, this is especially true in its punk
version. In most cases, though, popular uses of "DIY" in contemporary advertising affirm the gendered division of labor in
the home. A web search on DIY returns results on hardware
and power tools aimed at men and plans for DIY jewelry or
Martha Stewart's DIY pumpkin-spice latte pitched to women.
Informal and inexpert by nature, straddling work and leisure,
DIY has typically never been a strict necessity: you don't just
"do it yourself" because you *have* to, but also, and sometimes
mostly, because you *want to*. More than a method of *doing* various
things, in the home and with your friends, DIY has become a
name for a way of being in the world, what the art theorist Lane
Relyea calls "a potent mix of entrepreneurial agency and networked sociality, proclaiming itself heir to both punk autonomy,
the notion of living by your wits and as an outsider, and to a sub-
cultural basis for authentic artistic production."[20] DIY's present
mixture of autonomous self-determination with entrepreneurial
self-reliance is what makes propositions like Merkel's so insidi-

ous. Rent-paying tenants of public housing have every right to expect their landlord to "do it" for them; in this case, the enthusiastic voluntarism of "do it yourself" has become more like an indifferent invitation to "do it your damn self." Is the prospect of student debt preventing you from pursuing higher education? Find a cheaper alternative with "DIY education" in the form of free online classes and Project Gutenberg.[21] Can't afford a home mortgage? Buy some land and build yourself a tiny house. DIY celebrates individualistic substitutes for state obligations or political solutions, like free public education or affordable housing. In this way, DIY can become, like the more politicized versions of artisanal and maker culture, a practice of consumption masquerading as a practice of citizenship.

ECOSYSTEM (N.)

Ecosystem is often used to describe a local network of businesses in a similar place, field, or complex supply chain ("Portland's **maker** ecosystem," the "Apple ecosystem," or at a greater level of abstraction, the "**innovation** ecosystem") or the internal culture of a particular organization ("Georgia Tech's innovation ecosystem"). Like many of what Margaret Brindle and Peter Stearns call "management enthusiasms," the concept of the business ecosystem compels a certain zeal in its adherents, but it is not particularly original or consistent. It recycles other ideas (the need to balance competitive and cooperative approaches, the importance of vigilance against **disruptors**, the entrepreneurial resistance to bureaucracy) in a new language of ecological balance.[1]

"Crack open an office building . . . from the late twentieth century," writes Michelle Murphy in *Sick Building Syndrome and the Problem of Uncertainty*, "and you will find a machine." These machines are built to offer what has, since the middle of the century, been known as "climate control," a phrase first used at the turn of the twentieth century by utopian fantasists to describe the dream of controlling the weather *outside*. By mid-century, climate control was focused more humbly on the indoors, and as Murphy argues, postwar office design set out to "produce a clean, orderly corporate world sealed off from both the polluted outdoors and the dangerous factory floor." Offices were designed to produce an environment that reflected capitalism as their designers imagined it: clean, organized, dynamic, and as complex as a living ecosystem—only more manageable.[2]

Beyond the obvious pleasures of air conditioning, the indoor spaces where office workers toiled had an added appeal. As models of a capitalist economy, climate-controlled offices made a pleasant contrast to the fields and factories these workers' mothers and fathers knew. Theories of organizational dynamics began to reflect the spatial model of an ordered, safe, and manageable business ecosystem. In the late 1970s, the concept of "organizational ecology," developed by the sociologists Michael T. Hannan and John Freeman, gave rise to biological and environmental analogies for the firm that have proliferated in management literature ever since. Business climate and corporate **synergy** barely register as biological metaphors anymore, so normalized have they become in economic language. "Incubators" nurture hatchling tech firms; one of these, in Austin, TX, is "a 'coral reef' for startups," as an author in the *Harvard Business Review* puts it. Speakers of business jargon invoke "green fields" and "blue skies" as metaphors of abundance. These models view the company as a network, whose parts are both fluid and responsive to planning, a contradictory unity of flexibility and control.[3]

James Moore's 1993 *Harvard Business Review* article, "Predators and Prey: A New Ecology of Competition," which is widely credited with popularizing the business ecosystem concept, exemplifies the contradictions of its strained environmental analogy. Business ecosystems "condense," Moore writes, from the "original swirl of capital," like the cosmos emerging from the Big Bang. Many of Moore's sentences have the following sort of "just as" construction: "Business ecosystems condense out of the original swirl of capital, customer interest, and talent generated by a new innovation," he writes, "just as successful species spring from the natural resources of sunlight, water, and soil nutrients." The analogy frays when one considers that the point of the concept is to advise executives how to manage the system in order to thrive in it.[4] In a business ecosystem, it turns out, the wiliest predators can game the system.

One can understand the appeal of this ecological model, regardless of how much biological sense it makes. The market understood this way is not the symbolically pitiless storm or inescapable octopus of nineteenth-century labor fiction; instead, it is a manageable, benevolent force of nature. Part of this shift is *ideological* in that word's limited, pejorative sense of an illusion that expresses the interests of a ruling class. Business ecologies naturalize a social system and make a crisis-prone economy seem as reliable as office air-conditioning. As Raymond Williams (and others) remind us, however, it is important to distinguish between ideology as a mere illusion and ideology as a form of consciousness.[5] This becomes important when we consider how the business ecosystem model navigates (as it were) the problem of environmental danger. As the actual ecology of the world outside becomes more imperiled, it seems to be no coincidence that the fantasy of a climate-controlled indoor business ecosystem becomes ever more attractive. And yet one major feature of outdoor ecosystems, after all, is their dangerous unpredictability—ask many people what they associate first with "ecosystems," and they might mention hurricanes, snakes, fire ants, what Melville called the "murderous thinkings" of the "unsounded deeps," etc. In the business ecosystem, though, strong leaders can always navigate metaphorical seas, shoals, or tempests. The "laws" of disruptive innovation, Clayton Christensen writes in *The Innovator's Dilemma*, "are so strong that managers who ignore or fight them are nearly powerless to pilot their companies through a disruptive technology storm."[6]

Nature's unpredictability is elegantly reframed in this literature either as the danger of competition, as in Christensen's work, or in more benign terms as "serendipity." "Like its natural equivalent," says Shirley Ann Jackson, president of Rensselaer Polytechnic Institute, "an innovation ecosystem depends on an intricate set of relationships to succeed." Jackson is a physicist by training and a university president by profession, so she deals rather fast and loose with the natural analogy at play here, to defend the rather unempirical virtue of "serendipity" as a driver of value creation. Serendipity she defines as the unintended re-sults of open-ended research and collaboration. Without it, the innovation ecosystem will wither and die.[7] Deborah Jackson, a physicist at the National Science Foundation and author of a widely-cited article defining the "innovation ecosystem," organ-izes her model of business dynamism around the interconnect-edness of a natural system. Critical to the analogy is the notion of "equilibrium," a state that an ecosystem, like an economy, tends to seek. An innovation is thought to be thriving, Jackson writes, "when the sources invested in the knowledge economy . . . are subsequently replenished by innovation induced profit increases in the commercial economy." When this happens, the ecosystem is in equilibrium. The first problem with this model is that, as other critics have observed, it relies on a teleological fallacy.[8] An innovation or business ecosystem is distinguished from any generic "system" only by its purpose—to innovate or to conduct business. The business ecosystem is less vibrant intellectual bio-sphere than airtight rhetorical tomb.

All of these analogies also rest on the unexamined assumption that innovation is the source of all value. One does not need to be a Marxist (although it helps) to see how the above biological anal-ogies render labor invisible, when it is not disposable. There are, in a workplace as in an ecosystem, competing models of health and thriving, after all: does economic health refer to the abundance, stability, safety, and rates of compensation of the jobs that most people do in that economy? Or does it mean wealth maximization for the owners of capital? Again, available ecological models of competition and growth—of predatory animals devouring prey, and dead vegetation decomposing to feed the living—complicate the idyll of an interconnected, serendipitous ecological system. "Ideally," Deborah Jackson writes, "the ecosystem is also struc-tured to recover and recycle resources (including **human capital**) that are released upon failure of an enterprise."[9] Ideally, worker, you will be recycled as metaphorical compost. Ecosystems, then, are a way of modeling capitalist economies as all things to all people: as complex but local, competitive yet serendipitous, as a perennial gale and a **resilient** garden. One thing ecosystems conspicuously aren't, though, is workplaces—that is, networks of power shaped by competing interests, by bosses and workers—predators and prey, you might say.

EMPOWERMENT (N.); EMPOWER (V.)

Like **sustainability**, empowerment is a concept once associated with the left which has been absorbed by many of the institutions it once set out to criticize. Its origins are complex and diverse: the empowerment concept can trace its genealogy to feminist theory, social work, African American civil rights discourse, third-world liberation theology, and critical studies of post-colonial development. It has been largely defanged as a term of oppositional politics, though, as it has become a popular marketing slogan, for both consumer products and politicians. The empowerment **brand** is aimed especially at women, where it signifies a feminism aligned with women's individual, material success.

The *OED* defines empowerment as "the fact or action of acquiring more control over one's life or circumstances through increased civil rights, independence, self-esteem, etc." As Anne-Emmanuèle Calvès writes in her history of the term in Global South development literature, empowerment began as a critique of foreign aid programs that emphasized economic growth as the benchmark of success. Growth-centered development, argued these critics, tended to be hierarchical and insensitive to the social dimension of economic change—to the real ways in which abstract economic conditions are lived on the ground and in the household. The critics' goal was to champion a more participatory alternative—to turn the *objects* of development into *subjects,* and to emphasize not only material deprivation, as charted by GDP and growth rates, but social, political, and cultural *disempowerment*. Feminist development critics in particular argued that women's work, often unwaged and unmeasured, was undervalued by conventional measures and practices of economic development.[10]

This vein in empowerment's history also draws on intellectual and political forebears like the radical Brazilian pedagogue Paolo Freire, who argued that structures of political domination produce a "dominated consciousness." Through a model of education as "concientization"—a revolutionary process of overcoming this conditioned domination—the student becomes aware of her place in the world and develops strategies to transform it. In the United States, Barbara Solomon's 1976 book *Black Empowerment: Social Work in Oppressed Communities* counterposed empowerment to "powerlessness," a system but crucially also a feeling of racial disadvantage, inferiority, or insignificance that derives from being a member of a stigmatized population in a white-dominated society. Solomon directed her book to what she calls the "helping professions," social workers, teachers, and others, who, she argued, must abandon paternalist attitudes and practices of service and treat clients as agents and partners in their own right. Echoing in her title the slogan of "Black Power," which she describes as a satisfying but vague theory, Solomon intended Black empowerment as a model of praxis.[11]

These disparate approaches to empowerment share a conviction that power operates not only through "macro" systems like national industrial policy, foreign aid, or great-power conflicts but through "micro" systems like the gendered division of labor in the household or the neighborhood school. However, in more recent uses of the term, Solomon's "powerlessness" and Freire's "dominated consciousness"—which both make a charge of deprivation, as if something rightfully one's own has been stolen or usurped—have tended to be replaced by more passive synonyms like "disempowerment" and "exclusion." It is now common to see "empowerment" in the mission statements of major financial and development organizations like the World Bank, the micro-lending Grameen Foundation, and the Organization for Economic Co-operation and Development (OECD). As Calvès argues, empowerment's critique of mainstream development's paternalism quickly became mainstream itself, and in the process, it became depoliticized. The OECD defines empowerment as "the capacity of women and men to participate in, contribute to and benefit from growth processes in ways which recognize the value of their contributions, respect their dignity and make it possible to negotiate a fairer distribution of the benefits of growth."[12] The implication is that "participation" by necessity yields "fairness": it is "exclusion" from participation in the economy, rather than the economy itself, that disempowers.

Today, empowerment is most common as a feminist concept—or at least as a brand identity alluding to feminism. Here as well, the discourse of empowerment is driven by a celebration of individual *participation* in structures of authority, and less by a critique of the structures themselves. The examples of corporate advertising that use some variation on women's empowerment as a marketing slogan are legion—there is empowerment underwear, soap, and even a feminist umbrella ("Empower yourself," it shouts to the skies). As Jia Tolentino argues in her survey of the word's popularity in advertising and what she terms "lightweight" corporate feminism, what arose as a critique of the insidious operation of power at the level of the street, the school, the home, and the body—grasping the political in the personal, in short—has become another way of disguising the political by exalting the personal. As Tolentino puts it, "'empowerment' invokes power while signifying the lack of it. It functions like an explorer staking a claim on a new territory with a white flag."[13]

Rhetorically foregrounding the agency of the oppressed—a laudable goal in the abstract—can have the effect of disguising that of the oppressor. This is not always unintended. Individualist notions of empowerment can be barely disguised euphemisms for economic deregulation. Empower the Poor, a Christian social-service organization in rural Virginia, declares that "a world without extreme poverty can be achieved through empowerment and not handouts," and boasts of teaching its impoverished clients "self-reliance." School **choice** policies that encourage market competition between public school districts and charter networks are also celebrated for "empowering" parents. Here, empowerment becomes insidious: if the power to choose between market-based options is yours, the responsibility for your child's school's failure becomes yours as well. In such ways empowerment rhetoric outsources the state's responsibility for education and poverty reduction to relatively *powerless* individuals, further burdening those whose liberation the concept was once meant to facilitate.[14]

"With power," wrote Stokely Carmichael in 1966, "the masses could *make or participate in making* the decisions which govern their destinies, and thus create basic change in their day-to-day lives."[15] Empowerment often functions quite differently than "power" does in Carmichael's formulation. It works individually and not collectively; its model of agency lies in consumption and not agitation; its horizon is participation, not justice. Unlike "equality" but much like "sustainability," there is no clear way to measure the success or failure of empowerment—just as a mining corporation could always be more **sustainable**, even a Facebook executive can always be more empowered than she already is. It has become a concept of liberation, in short, that no one is against—making it a powerless concept indeed.

ENGAGEMENT (N.)

"Community engagement" and "civic engagement" are phrases that first appear in printed English sometime in the mid-1950s, according to Google's ngram database. One might naively assume that the concept of engagement only became popular once everyone noticed it missing. Yet the basic problems these phrases seem to respond to—political atomization and fraying community ties—are not new or unique to our times. What particular meaning, then, does the word "engagement" have for us now?

The term "civic engagement" was popularized by the political scientist Robert Putnam's influential 1995 book, *Bowling Alone: The Collapse and Revival of American Community*, which argued that American civic life had deteriorated over the last third of the twentieth century. Putnam argued that Americans had become less likely to join community organizations, from the PTA to the Elks to bowling leagues, and more likely to join passively when they do, by writing an annual check or signing a petition. "Social capital," the social relations that have value in shaping reciprocal obligations within a community, is a term Putnam uses roughly synonymously with civic engagement. Social capital, Putnam writes, is the value of social relationships among individuals. It can be private and public, but social capital is richest, he says, when it is "embedded in a dense network of reciprocal social relations."[16] The concept of social capital exemplifies the broader trend many of these keywords document: the modeling of moral and social interactions on the **market**. One goes to church to acquire salvation, fellowship, and "social capital," and not necessarily in that order.

Civic engagement is said to be on the decline, and yet we seem more and more "engaged" by institutions, **brands**, and anyone else who claims to want our attention. The *OED* gives a broad set of definitions for "engage" and "engagement," but all of them involve some sense of a formal covenant, a contract, or a conflict: the marriage contract, some other legal agreement, or a military battle. However, it's hard to find a dictionary meaning that suits the way many civic institutions routinely use the word: as consensual participation. Some obsolete definitions point to the talents of charm: "To attach by pleasing qualities; to attract, charm, fascinate." "If you engage his heart," wrote the Earl of Chesterfield in 1751 in a letter offering advice on social niceties to his son, "you have a fair chance for imposing upon his understanding." The network of affections that Putnam's "civic engagement" summons for us actually belongs to obsolete meanings: "the fact of being entangled," for example, last common in the sixteenth century. But even this definition carried with it a negative connotation that is absent from our contemporary connotation of voluntary association for mutual benefit.[17]

For a specific example, let's look at *Detroit Future City*, the strategic framework for the city's planners, released in 2012 after four years of research. The project drew on the technical expertise of urban planners from around the country and was shaped decisively, or so the report claims, by the "engagement" of average Detroiters. The plan's basic premise is that given Detroit's vast surplus of idle public land, property development and the attraction of entrepreneurial investment will be the material basis of the future city. From the beginning of the report, one can read an anxiety about anticipated criticism of the urban planning process by a citizenry with a deep historical memory of destructive urban renewal initiatives. *Detroit Future City* incorporated numerous public events into the planners' research with this history in mind. However, Joshua Akers, a geographer at University of Michigan–Dearborn, recounts how embattled this "engagement" process often was in practice. After the first open meetings drew large crowds angry about poor city services, later events were more stage-managed: emcees ran the floor, and attendees were given clickers that allowed them to "vote" on choices presented to them: did they think that education, for example, was their neighborhood's greatest priority, or was it jobs or transportation?[18] Certainly, any move away from authoritarian models of planning is laudable. However, what often happened in practice, argues Akers, is that community "engagement" was managed to suit expert models, rather than the expert models being shaped by popular participation. Engagement as "participation" suggests a dynamic, two-way exchange, but Lord Chesterfield's motivated seduction is clear in the DFC's own explanation of their term: "Why engage?" the authors ask. You might wonder why a plan for an ostensibly democratic polity even has to ask, but here's what they say:

> Civic engagement yields lasting benefits. This is true of any development endeavor or long-term initiative, including the Detroit Strategic Framework. Here's why: first, civic engagement helps strengthen and expand the base of support for a given effort. More people become informed, activated and mobilized through engagement efforts. Opposition is less likely because concerns are addressed within the process.[19]

One can read this as a promise that planners, acting in good faith, will willingly incorporate public concerns into their decisions. If

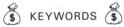

you're skeptical about that, a less generous reading would suggest that engagement is valuable because it blunts opposition. The point of engagement then becomes making the public feel involved in decisions that others will ultimately make.

If civic engagement really is in decline in America, as Putnam claimed in *Bowling Alone*, one thing that is not in decline is the ritualistic performance of civic engagement. The circuses of political elections in the United States are only the most obvious case in point. In one populist breath, we routinely condemn the corruption of politicians who, it is said, never listen to the average voter. And in the next, we harangue the average voter for failing to participate in a process we routinely describe as corrupted. Perhaps, rather than criticizing the public's "disengagement" as the absence of engagement, we should focus instead on the institutions that give us so many good reasons to disengage in the first place.

ENTREPRENEUR, ENTREPRENEURSHIP (N.)

Entrepreneur combines the pixie dust of **innovation**, the social conscience of the **stakeholder**, the versatile vagueness of **nimble**, and, with its French derivation, a touch of the glamour that "businessman," "capitalist," or "manager" can never approach. The popularity of entrepreneurship amplifies the celebration of **leaders** over labor, of individualism over solidarity. Its cultish prominence in contemporary capitalist culture is such that it is regularly requisitioned into a stream of cumbersome portmanteaus, each more absurd than the last, like "authorpreneur," "teacherpreneur," and "pastorpreneur." It is no surprise that in an age of austerity, when most people's sense of control over their lives is contracting—due to indebtedness, precarious employment, or lack of employment altogether—that there should emerge a hero who stands for agency, material success, and moral determination all at once. Derived from the French verb *entreprendre,* "to undertake," the "entrepreneur" is the masculine noun form of the verb—literally "one who undertakes something." It's critical that the word is a third-person verb deriva-tion, since some individualized action is always implied, even as "entrepreneurial" has come to describe the routine workings of ever-more complex bureaucracies. Entrepreneurs *do* things—important, good, world-changing things. This points to an im-portant evolution in the word's usage since its popularization in the 1930s, which is the development of its current air of virtue, even zealotry.

The first major theorist of entrepreneurship as such was Joseph Schumpeter, who emphasized the difference between the "cap-italist" and the "entrepreneur." Schumpeter's definition of the latter was closely linked to his influential theory of innovation, which he understood historically, as a process of economic trans-formation that was both destructive and progressive. For Marx and Engels, the process of capitalist accumulation "has been the first to show what man's activity can bring about." For Marx, of course, the author of this revolutionary transformation was a class—the bourgeoisie—and its method was exploitation. For Schumpeter, the historical process of capitalism was also **creative** and it was driven not by a class, but by an individual character he called "the entrepreneur." In *The Theory of Economic Development*, he wrote, "the carrying out of new combinations [by which Schumpeter refers to production processes] we call 'enterprise'; the individuals whose function it is to carry them out we call 'entrepreneurs.'" In *Capitalism, Socialism, and Democracy* (1942), which has remained influential in management training circles for its concept of "creative destruction," Schumpeter describes innovation as "the entrepreneurial function":

> [T]o reform or revolutionize the pattern of production by exploiting an invention or, more generally, an untried tech-nological possibility for producing a new commodity or pro-ducing an old one in a new way, by opening up a new source of supply of materials or a new outlet for products, by reor-ganizing an industry and so on.[20]

For Schumpeter, then, the "entrepreneur" is the agent of inno-vation. His definition of the entrepreneur's role is somewhat abstract, as Schumpeter himself acknowledges. Being the historical agent for capitalism's creative, world-making turbulence is hard to quantify or professionalize, and therefore to assess or teach, a point lost on many of his contemporary disciples. Moreover, because entrepreneurship is a function for Schumpeter and not a social class or a profession, an "entrepreneur" is not the same as the "capitalist" or the "manager." The entrepreneur does not control capital or the means of production; instead, the entrepreneur is a functionary, but a somewhat heroic one, one who has the power to restrain the deadening effects of monopoly and unleash the power of creative destruction. Schumpeterian innovation thus contains a central paradox: it is both a historical force and a personal quality.

Among critics of this social type, Marxists have had little to say about entrepreneurs as such, with exceptions like E. P. Thompson, in *The Making of the English Working Class,* who viewed entrepreneurs as synonymous with "middlemen." Elsewhere he used the word in the same breath as "rentier," a non-productive profiteer.[21] The economist Paul Sweezy, in a sympathetic assessment of Schumpeter's theory of innovation, was one exception. Sweezy accepted Schumpeter's thesis of innovation as a force of transformation in capitalist production, but he rejected the centrality he gave to individual agency. It is not "innovation" as a process to which Sweezy objects, but the entrepreneurial "innovator" as an archetype driving the process. Rather than Schumpeter's character of the autonomous entrepreneur powering the economy's movement, wrote Sweezy, "we may instead regard the typical innovator as the tool of the social relations in which he is enmeshed and which force him to innovate on pain of elimination." In those last four words Sweezy alludes to Marx's description in the *Manifesto* of the hard bargain driven by the bourgeoisie as it traverses the globe. In other words, for Sweezy, it is capital accumulation—not the entrepreneurial function— that drives "creative destruction."[22]

Others have defined the entrepreneur as the "risk-taker," but this is pure mystification, given the romance attached to the bold, the fearless, the gambling man.[23] Schumpeter himself insisted that the ultimate financial risk belongs to the owner of the means of production, who may not be an "entrepreneur" at all. While "entrepreneur" is now often used promiscuously for anyone who owns a business, some version of a functional distinction between the capitalist and the entrepreneur persists in the term's popular usage. A Wall Street banker is rarely an entrepreneur in the business press; a tech mogul, no matter how successful, usually is. Clearly, some of this has to do with the entrepreneur's association with commerce—an entrepreneur sells a product or a service. Yet bankers sell services, and one can hardly accuse Wall Street bankers of failing to innovate sophisticated processes of doing whatever it is they do. More important than the commercial meaning of entrepreneur, which is highly variable and subjective, is its residual moral signification. The myth of the entrepreneur exhibits a Weberian "spirit of capitalism," the pursuit of virtue through the accumulation of wealth. It also bears the traces of innovation's origins as a term of political and religious dissent. The entrepreneur pursues a calling and rebels against orthodoxy—"moves fast and breaks things," as Mark Zuckerberg famously said—while the capitalist merely makes money. The zealous pursuit of a higher calling (in Facebook's case, making the world "more open and connected") makes the founder of Facebook an entrepreneur. This is the difference, between "entrepreneur*ship*" and "business." According to Google's ngram database, "entrepreneurship" skyrocketed between 2000 and 2010 but only began to appear in earnest around mid-century, making it a much newer concept than "entrepreneur." The elevation of Schumpeter's professional type to our social calling, therefore, is new.

"Entrepreneurship" is more than "business"—it is a way of life. Weber argued in *The Protestant Ethic and the Spirit of Capitalism* that American capitalism gave the impulse to seek profit the virtue of a vocation or a "calling."[24] But has that ethic ever been embodied in such a singular archetype as "the entrepreneur" of today? Earlier eras, of course, lionized "self-made men" and cap-

tains of industry. Henry Ford may have been a capitalist role
model, but whatever social good he was said to have done came
from the particular product he built, not from his impulse to
build *anything*. For Ford, meeting some higher social goal (preserving old barns, advancing the cause of fascism) was an eccentric side project, rather than the main goal of his enterprise. But
the *Wall Street Journal*'s handbook for entrepreneurs, *The Complete
Small Business Guidebook*, shows how a zealous sense of vocation
is routinely folded into the entrepreneurial function. The book
makes entrepreneurship sound almost monastic in the sacrifices
it demands of believers. It advises novices entering the faith that
"it's unwise to start down the path of entrepreneurship unless
you've got a zeal that will get you through rough patches and
keep you interested long after the initial enthusiasm has faded."
In this excerpt, you may read this as a story of a man who set off
unprepared upon the lonely path of righteousness, was tested,
and then redeemed:

> Working seven days a week, losing touch with friends, aban-
> doning old hobbies and interests and not making time for
> loved ones can quickly lead to burnout in the midst of starting
> up—and ultimately to business failure. That's what happened
> to James Zimbardi, an entrepreneur in Orlando, Florida,
> who . . . started his first company in 1997 and worked as hard
> as possible, for as long as possible, until his creativity, enthu-
> siasm and energy were sapped. By 2002, he was a broken
> man—the business took a downturn, and so did his personal
> life. Now Zimbardi is at work on his second company, Allgen
> Financial Services, and sticking to better habits to maintain
> work/life balance, such as not working on Sundays, making
> time for hobbies such as sailing and salsa dancing, and build-
> ing close ties with other business owners through a faith-
> based support network.[25]

Note that even the *Wall Street Journal* doesn't hold out material rewards for the new, no-longer broken James Zimbardi. He
didn't go into business for Cadillacs or a college fund. He did it
for the zeal.

In 2012, *CBS Evening News* profiled Richard Branson, the Virgin founder who has personified the entrepreneurship fantasy of artistic "vision" and moral zeal. Branson might be most accurately described as "investor," but "entrepreneur" is more than a mere professional function—it is Branson's personal **brand** and something like a code. Everything he does, from direct music sales to founding an airline, is an expression of his "values," not the mere desire to increase his capital. This moral sense lends itself easily to "social entrepreneurship," which the Charles Schwab Foundation for Social Entrepreneurship defines in part as the drive to "pursue poverty alleviation . . . with entrepreneurial zeal." A social entrepreneur is a "pragmatic visionary" who "innovates by finding a new product, a new service, or a new approach to a social problem." The final trait, however, is the real coup de grace: "Combines the characteristics represented by Richard Branson and Mother Teresa."[26]

The portraits of Virgin's executive roster on the company website show a succession of middle-aged white men in open-collared shirts tucked into blue jeans, a uniform of corporate casualness. Amidst the blue-jeaned men you will find the firm's only female executive, Jean Oelwang, who runs "Virgin Unite," the company's "entrepreneurial foundation," the word "entrepreneurial" filling in where "charitable" might once have sufficed. There's talk of developing "new approaches to social and environmental issues," approaches which include the "Branson Centres of Entrepreneurship." So Virgin's entrepreneurship yields its foundation for entrepreneurship, which addresses environmental crisis, through its own brand of entrepreneurship. It is unclear where, or even if, the business ends and the charity begins. Oelwang's bio includes among her qualifications her work as a "VISTA volunteer where she worked with—and learned from—homeless teens in Chicago." No telling what she learned from them, but the turn to youth here signals one of the cult of entrepreneurship's key growth areas, education. Entrepreneurship summer camps, for example, promise to teach business success to children as young as five. While some offer practical lessons on things like writing a business plan, their real emphasis is cultivating the elusive "entrepreneurial spirit," as a recent article on the camps in the *Wall Street Journal* put it. "Children are born imaginative, energetic, and willing to take risks," a reporter noted, "but lose this entrepreneurial spirit." Children's imagination and creativity, as it turns out, are merely unrefined pre-professional skills. Not only is children's free time reconfigured as wasted labor-hours, but education itself is reduced to pre-professionalization. One entrepreneurial camp, named SuperCamp, begins its pitch ominously, by pressing on parents' sense of dread about a jobless future: "The challenges facing students ahead are mounting," warns the camp director. "We now have a global economy where market competition—nationally and internationally—is fierce." Anxiety, here, becomes opportunity. Higher education plays on this marketable sense of professional anxiety—a more proximate concern for college students—while advancing a similar vision of education as naturally entrepreneurial, and ideally profit-making. In 2017, NYU dedicated desks in its library "for entrepreneurial purposes only," warning students that they were for "working on your startup, not your homework." And Michigan State has emblazoned benches on campus with the slogan, "To a Spartan, this isn't a bench—it's an idea generator," lest any students be tempted to waste an unproductive minute daydreaming.[27]

Entrepreneurship education is not just for elite college students or the comfortable children of the suburban middle class, however. Indeed, the model of education as managerial training may ironically be one of the most egalitarian aspects of American public education, insofar as it has spread across the class and racial boundaries of city and suburb. The fierceness of the competition spreads from leafy suburban Pittsburgh to inner-city Cleveland, where an entrepreneurship preparatory school opened in 2006. Never mind that some children might not want to grow up to run a business, that some might rather be teachers or mechanics, or even nothing in particular just yet; forget that imagination and creativity might be something other than a source of wealth.

The cult of entrepreneurship's commodification of imagination, its celebration of self-sacrifice, and its bootstraps individualism make it a perfect ethic for social disinvestment masquerading as reform and profiteering disguised as charity. Entrepreneurship means that now you're on your own, kid.

EXCELLENCE (N.)

"Excellence" is one of the few words in this list that has actually been in decline over the last two centuries, according to Google's ngram data. This is because the aristocracies to which "excellence" once pertained have also been in decline. (Or perhaps we just have new words for them.) The word has most often been applied to great men and particularly esteemed achievements. The noun is superlative: excellence is not merely good, it is superior. As the *OED* puts it, it indicates "good qualities in an eminent or unusual degree." "Excellency" was thus an honorific bestowed on such excellent persons, whose excellence was conferred at birth. For this reason, in a democratic society, excellence should be anachronistic, if not oxymoronic: everybody cannot be eminent in an unusual degree, by definition.

In spite of this overall decline, the word proliferates in a variety of fields, from advertising and athletics to primary, secondary, and higher education. Excellence entered the education lexicon with the 1983 publication of the landmark report, *A Nation at Risk,* issued by a Reagan White House-appointed blue-ribbon commission. The report warned darkly of national educational decline and corresponding national weakness as a "common culture" and even "the honorable word, 'patriotism'" receded. The commission's emphasis on refining national academic standards has proven durable over the decades since, but one of its major rationales for standardization was cultural and implicitly racial: "rigor" has been displaced by tribal "social" concerns encouraged by post-1960s multiculturalism, the authors wrote. By calling for by-now familiar curatives like "measurable standards," and some unfamiliar ones like higher pay for teachers, *A Nation at Risk* mixed the quaintly old (its justification of education as the crafting of a national culture) and the technocratically new (education to make the nation economically competitive globally). The path to each of these goals, the civic and the economic, was the path of excellence, which the commission defined in various ways. "At the level of the *individual learner,*" went one definition, excellence "means performing on the boundary of individual ability in ways that test and push back personal limits, in school and in the workplace." At the level of an institution and a society, excellence refers to the high expectations and the incentives for meeting and pushing these boundaries.[28]

Excellence, in other words, is the pursuit of excellence.[29] A common thread among terms like **accountability**, **innovation**, and **resilience** is this tendency to tautology. This is because such terms often have no independent meaning outside of the approving circles of their own circulation. Their meanings "float," intelligible in terms of themselves or some synonym. As a result, excellence is often accused of being an empty platitude when it is not derided as a form of undercover elitism. In the former instance, it has suffered what linguists call "semantic bleaching"— the weakening of its meaning over time. As a result, "excellent" now means "very good," rather than "eminent," as Kathryn Allen observes in her essay on the word's history. But at the same time, the primary meaning of "eminent" still adheres to the word. As a result, it's not always clear what policy makers, administrators, and bosses of all kinds mean when they demand excellence: do they mean excelling—beating the competition, achieving a superior standard compared to others? Or do they mean working at a consistent level across the board—such that everyone achieves some measure of "very good"? The political implications of this paradox are most apparent in education, where "excellence," an essentially comparative term, is treated as an absolute. If all students are expected to achieve excellence, what does excellence mean, if not "average"? Perhaps it is not so surprising that excellence has found a home in a field that is, in theory, committed to nurturing an egalitarian ideal of democratic citizenship but is, in practice, also defined by ranking and hierarchy in the form of grades, school prestige, and so forth. The pursuit of "excellence" reconciles these competing ideals without having to recognize them as competing.[30]

In his critique of what he called the "university of excellence," Bill Readings argued that excellence was worse than a meaningless platitude: rather, its meaninglessness was part of its power. Its vagueness was consequential for those eager to detach the purpose of education from notions of citizenship or other imperatives that cannot be reduced to consumer products.[31] Instead, all that matters is success, as measured by prestige and various financial metrics. Excellence serves only itself.

FAIL (V., N.); FAILURE (N.)

Failure has taken on multiple meanings in political journalism and business ideology in recent years. There is the foreign-policy intellectual hobbyhorse of the "failed state," in which the passive voice describes the immiseration of postcolonial nations that show up on such lists. More recent still is the celebration of failure in **entrepreneurship** discourse, where it is closely related to **innovation**. There, failure is a veritable fountain of obvious metaphors. Out of failure springs innovation. Failure is innovation's foundation. Failure drives innovation. Failure is the mother of innovation. This embrace of failure offers reassurance, celebrating hard work and persistence but granting that these do not always pay off. The business journalist Adam Davidson penned an article in praise of this meaning of "failure" in the *New York Times Magazine* in 2017, breezing through the history of capitalism (without ever using the word) as a series of daring risks by entrepreneurs unafraid to tempt failure. Davidson decries the "proselytizing" associated with the voguish discourse of innovation, without realizing that the seemingly counterintuitive embrace of failure is part of the proselytizing script. Indeed, innovation as he uses the term is not a deity one worships but more like a spirit of progress marching across the generations. Failure, or the ability to risk it, is one of its driving forces.[1]

Such defenses of "failing" make logical sense, as clichés often do: if at first you don't succeed, try, try again, and whatever doesn't kill you only makes you stronger, and so on. (Or as Davidson puts it: "terror...can be helpful.") On the business websites where the literature of failure spreads, articles draw on many of the same anecdotes: 3M's ineffective glue that became the basis of Post-it notes, the unexpectedly lucrative side effects of an overlooked blood-pressure drug called Viagra. Failures are not gambles or consequences of an unfair system, but temporary setbacks in a basically fair order that can prepare you for later success. One Oakland private school has built an appreciation of failure into its kindergarten "innovation and **design**" curriculum, reframing a primary-school lesson about the importance of persistence as necessary training for the knowledge-economy job market.[2] Entrepreneurship's celebration of failure assumes a storyline that eventually ends in triumph. In so doing, it softens the well-known fact about starting a business: most entrepreneurial ventures will fail. Instead of debt, anxiety, and poverty, though, the failure narrative spins the likeliest outcome of starting a business as a deeper reserve of knowledge and **grit** for your next attempt. Davidson's warning about proselytizing aside, failure fits into the moralistic framework of so much innovation and entrepreneurship rhetoric in the business media. Entrepreneurship failure stories, like Christian conversion narratives, celebrate sacrifice and self-reliance, with hubris turned to humility after wandering through a wilderness of lost venture capital funding. One such anecdote describes a failed Silicon Valley entrepreneur, an overconfident wild success at a young age, before his business tanked and his investors abandoned him. Humbled, he started a new company called "Epiphany."[3]

In the foreign-policy shop, what is the opposite of "failed," as in "failed state"? The question is never asked, of course, since the concept simply assumes as the normative standard of development the countries (the United States and Western Europe) where the concept originates. Entrepreneurship failure, like failed-state failure, presumes a normative model of success, the justice of which is never questioned. If you succeed, it is because you deserved it—and presumably because you paid your dues in failures. And if we say that Congo has failed at development, to say that the United States, Britain, and Belgium have, by contrast, won development would be to admit that the whole business is a rigged contest, rather than a fair, shared endeavor. In the vernacular of the internet, by contrast, "fail" has been used ironically, never used with the reverence that characterizes so much entrepreneurship rhetoric. There, the opposite of the noun fail is "win." Why not "success" or "victory"? The answer, I think, is that both "failing" and "winning" ironize the competitiveness and atomization that are built into both the culture of social media and the cult of entrepreneurship. The epic fail ironizes the world-spanning, ostensibly innovative internet as a conventionally unfair, intrinsically silly object. But this remains an ironic exception to the rule of failure in the language of capitalism. The celebration of failure, instead of vindicating the underdog, is another way of venerating the winners.

FLEXIBLE (ADJ.); FLEXIBILITY (N.)

Flexibility has a history in the economic study of "labor flexibility," but aside from this rather technical usage, it is a common example of what I described in the introduction as late-capitalist body-talk—the modeling of firms and economies on the agility and strength of the human body.[4] In many of the keywords explored here, we have seen how imaginative, even fanciful, is the language of MBAs, business journalists, and economists, whose prestige derives in large part from their disciplines' pretensions to practical hard-headedness. One example of this literary bent in business journalism and economics is the frequent use of personifications for the otherwise impersonal **market.** There is the notion of "business confidence," in which abstractions like "the market" are given the fragile psyches of a lily-livered moper who must be driven back to cheerfulness. Along with the personification of a national economy in a single psychology is its metaphorical appearance as a human body. A firm cutting its budget ("trimming the fat") is getting **leaner, nimbler,** more **robust,** and ultimately more flexible. Austerity culture seems to demand a sort of embodied moral discipline, like that of the ascetic in the wilderness: trimmed of excess bulk, devoted to a single task, scornful of leisure that might detract from it.

Like those other bodily metaphors, flexibility is often used euphemistically in journalism, marketing, and political rhetoric. It can be pluralized as "flexibilities" to refer to different ways in which a firm or an individual worker can adjust to meet the demands of the market.[5] Wisconsin's Republican Governor Scott Walker has used the singular and plural forms of the word to promote environmental deregulation—a constriction upon flexibilities. One state bill provides "flexibilities in the disposal of oil absorbent materials" and allows government agencies "flexibility in maintaining pollution standards." Here, the word's euphemistic meaning should be clear enough—flexibility in pollution standards simply means looser pollution standards.[6] Flexibility as Walker uses it here is a metaphorical application of the common meaning, "freedom from stiffness or rigidity." Two obsolete definitions in the *OED* are telling, given the word's adoption by austerity-minded politicians and cost-cutting executives: "The quality of yielding to pressure" and the "readiness to yield to influence or persuasion, pliancy of mind or disposition." While flexibility as freedom calls to mind an athlete's dexterity, the latter definitions play on the word's most literal definition, an object's pliancy. Flexibility means freedom through "versatility," a quality said to inhere in the private market and in the digital technologies that often serve as a proxy for it. Besides versatility, the ability to do anything, flexibility also suggests capriciousness, the willingness to bend and yield as required.

For example, the phrase "flexible scheduling" has two radically different meanings based on the class position of the employee hearing it: in white-collar professions, it means revised hours, telecommuting, or part-time employment, offered as a benefit to employees with family obligations.[7] In retail and food service, however, "flexible scheduling" means something completely different: the rigid management of hourly wage workers' schedules by their bosses. This is what the Retail Action Project, borrowing a term from lean manufacturing in the automobile industry, calls "just-in-time scheduling."[8] Sophisticated scheduling software allows managers to plan their employees' schedules days or hours in advance, calibrating them to respond immediately to the smallest fluctuations in demand for labor. Here, it is the employees' time that is made flexible, not the firm's, and workers who want to maintain school commitments, family responsibilities, or even regular free time away from work must bend into shape. Flexible employees, who are ostensibly "free" from managerial pressure to conform to a standard working day, are in fact valued insofar as they assimilate to it.

Where nimble and lean refer to the shape, size, and expenditures of a firm, invoking austerity rhetoric's moral sanction against "waste," flexibility refers specifically to the ways in which time, compensated and otherwise, is commodified and controlled. A **nimble** organization maximizes productivity while minimizing labor costs, but it also requires flexible employees who can bend into as many different shapes as possible. The body-talk of contemporary capitalism imagines corporate businesses as bodies in virtually every way except as a group of overextended or underpaid ones. Those who invoke flexibility in earnest typically imagine themselves as great pragmatists, quantifying **competencies** wherever and whatever they may be. Less moralistic than nimble and less prophetic than **innovation**, the always ill-defined concept of flexibility celebrates a class-bound versatility. With flexibility and the right software, our bosses can conquer time and bend it to their will—and bend us, their subordinates, as well.

FREE (ADJ.)

Freedom is, to say the least, a broad subject, and to define it satisfactorily far exceeds the capacity of such a book as this. Instead, let us examine a few of the most common political and economic uses to which the adjective "free" has been recently put.

The most important is perhaps the "free **market**," meaning "an economic system in which prices are determined by unrestricted competition between privately owned businesses," according to the *OED*. But of course, no such purely unregulated economy exists, except in the daydreams of libertarians and oligarchs; in this respect, the "free market" describes an idea rather than a system. Its current dominance, as a neutral alternative to the more politically marked term "capitalism," became widespread around the middle of the twentieth century. "Free trade" is an older concept; though it now describes a regime of capital mobility otherwise shorthanded as "globalization" or "neoliberalism," a different demand for "free trade" dominated political debates and shaped revolutionary programs in Europe's nineteenth-century empires. "Free labor" also belongs to the nineteenth century, when in the United States it described an ideal of an autonomous laborer, working for himself in the farm, shop, and house, free to sell his labor when he chose and "asking no favors of capital on the one hand nor of hired laborers or slaves on the other," as Abraham Lincoln put it.[9] And then there is "free speech" (or "freedom of speech," as it is called in the US Bill of Rights), a hotly contested, regularly abused term of political and intellectual liberty.

It was in the aftermath of the Second World War that the "free market" emerged as a popular substitute for "capitalism," which had become compromised by socialist criticism and wartime planning during the preceding two decades. As the war turned against the Axis powers, the question in the United States of the postwar transition, or "reconversion," loomed large. Thus a 1944 headline in *Life* asked, "Reconversion to what? It used to be called 'capitalism.' By any name its basis is the 'free market.'" The article lays out a by-now familiar ideal of a free market that is a condition and also an expression of inalienable political rights, of freedom in the political and even existential senses: "The freer the market, the freer every man's **choice** as to what he will work at as well as what he will buy." These choices, in turn, make political freedoms possible:

> The free market is the only economic system now which Americans can safely count to increase their standard of living, release their own creative energy, use their resources ef-

ficiently, govern the infinitely complex jungle of their daily trading and protect their political democracy, all at the same time.

Some years later, the economist Milton Friedman developed this hopeful claim. In his 1962 book *Capitalism and Freedom,* Friedman described the free market, by which he meant a lightly-regulated form of capitalism, as the "means toward" political freedom. As Friedman concedes, however, sometimes economically free societies are politically unfree, the United States's enemies in World War II being a central example. Here, the free market is more than just an idea—it's an act of faith in a deliverance yet to come. Economic freedom is the *means* toward political freedom—nobody said how long it would take. In the time it takes for the arc of history to bend toward justice, though, you might as well get paid.[10]

Many uses of "free speech," meanwhile, use the adjective in a similarly idealized way, to describe something or someone that is essentially unburdened by structural or other constraints. Think of the recently popular journalistic hobbyhorse in which college campuses are invoked as treasured places of ideological neutrality, where all ideas, even objectionable, deeply unpopular ones, should compete in the "marketplace of ideas." Such versions of "free speech" modeled on a competitive marketplace ignore the very market forces that determine our ability to communicate: the consolidation of mass media, certain speakers' privileged access to it, and the economic penalty that many workers face if they use their free speech rights in a way that offends their employers. "Freedom of speech" is, moreover, a deceptively metaphorical phrase—that is, "speech" does not mean the act of talking, but communication in a broad sense, either through the media or in formal live settings. The metaphor often misleads the shallower thinkers on this subject into thinking of the principle of "free speech" as something governed by the etiquette of face-to-face, peer-to-peer **conversation**—hence the routine emphasis, irrelevant as a legal and political question, on civility and tone in many discussions of free speech controversies. These uses of free, therefore, betray an idealized overemphasis on the transcendent power of individual actions, and a corresponding underemphasis on institutional constraints, shared rights, and collective aspirations. In short, they are indicative of a general obliviousness about power and an indifference to the ways it is exercised.

G

GRIT (N.)

In a co-op grocery store in Philadelphia's University City situated between an Ivy League university and the rest of majority Black, working-class west Philadelphia, I stood restlessly in line behind a woman whose black t-shirt scolded me for my impatience. "GRIT," her shirt shouted in all caps, directing its ideal of scabrous determination at me and my basket of seltzer water and soy-based meat substitutes.

The other side of her t-shirt revealed that she had just gotten off work at the KIPP charter network, where grit is an organizing principle—practically an ideology. KIPP operates in mostly urban communities of color like west Philadelphia, with a distinctive educational philosophy that emphasizes "character," which at KIPP is divided into a taxonomy of seven virtues or "strengths." "To succeed in college and the world beyond," says the KIPP website, students "need both a strong academic foundation and well-developed character strengths." The value I was studying in line at the grocery store is among the most influential both inside and outside of the KIPP curricula, thanks to its voguish popularity in contemporary self-help literature. The *OED* defines "grit" as "firmness or solidity of character" and "indomitable spirit or pluck." KIPP calls it "**passion** and perseverance for long-term goals," a definition first developed by Angela Duckworth, a psychologist at the University of Pennsylvania, KIPP consultant, and author of the 2017 best-seller *Grit: The Power of Passion and Perseverance*. In the scholarly paper where she first defined her use of the concept, Duckworth wrote, "Grit entails working strenuously toward challenges maintaining effort and interest over years despite failure, adversity, and plateaus in progress." Her passion-based meaning of grit has the air of a new idea, but it is the newest twist on the old story of American middle-class moral reform for the poor, a modern version of the familiar bootstraps ideology of self-reliance.[1]

The concept's association with perseverance is not new—grit's primary meaning describes coarse sand and the *OED* dates the character metaphor to nineteenth-century US slang. One of its earliest literary usages as "indomitable spirit or pluck" comes from Nathaniel Hawthorne's 1863 English travel book, *Our Old Home*, where Hawthorne describes a sweet, delicate, but rather ineffectual English poet he meets as "deficient in grit." The *OED*'s use of "pluck" to describe this character trait is a revealing clue to grit's history. "Pluck" has a decidedly old-fashioned ring, and if it sounds like something Horatio Alger would say, that's because it's in the title of five of his novels. "Pluck" was one of Alger's favored synonyms for the working-class qualities of rugged determination, as Ethan Ris writes in his study of grit's history in American educational thought. Grit and pluck worked together; where pluck referred to the emotional trait of "heart," grit emphasizes "will," or what Alger, in the opening pages of *Grit, or the Young Boatman of Pine Point,* called "unusual firmness." This novel's fifteen-year old hero, Harry Morris, was a Mainer "sure to make his way in the world," Alger writes in explaining his nickname, "and maintain his rights against all aggression."[2] Alger's tales of city urchins and rural scamps—poor boys who earned their "grit" and "pluck" in their hard upbringing—were meant as examples for the soft sons of privilege, the primary audience for Alger's books.

KIPP counts Duckworth as a principal consultant, but today's pluckless men and women are a target audience for her book. Like many self-help books, Duckworth's *Grit* recapitulates familiar bromides in a new way: her lessons about hard work, dedication, and success come with new data, terminology, and the sheen of science. Duckworth's grit is not the masculine quality of Alger and Hawthorne. But what Alger calls "strength of will" bears some resemblance to her own "perseverance." She might also find value in "pluck," since as she has pointed out, what is overlooked by critics of her theory of grit is its emphasis on passion.[3] In fact, Duckworth's grit is a combination of Alger's grit and pluck: unusual firmness as well as heart. Duckworth's grit is also egalitarian, defined (as Alger's also was) against notions of success as hereditary or class-bound. She defines grit against "genius," which she considers (quite reasonably) to be elitist and unambitious—a faith in the singular genius of others, she says, is an excuse for our own complacency. Introducing the book with what we must call a humble-brag anecdote about winning a MacArthur "genius" grant but disapproving of its popular name, she disavows the label as ill-conceived. "What we eventually accomplish may depend more on our passion and perseverance than on our innate talent," she writes, establishing her book's major theme. Grit is an underdog's attribute, which disproves myths of innate ability, and the class, race, or national attributes often thought to correlate with it.

However, grit's class markings are not far beneath the surface of its contemporary populism. And it is no coincidence, as Ris points out, that the moral ideal of grit thrives in decades of pronounced inequality—Alger's Gilded Age at the end of the nineteenth century and our own at the beginning of the twenty-first.[4] In one sense, the difference between late nineteenth-century and early twenty-first century grit is a simple reversal of terms: while it is no longer politically acceptable to describe the poor as "sullen" or lacking in "sobriety" and "industry," it is acceptable, and even progressive, to propose teaching their children "zest," "self-control," and "grit," all KIPP "character strengths."[5] Instead of deriding the poor for lacking it, we say that they need it and have the power to learn it.

While the policy applications of "grit" mostly fall on urban public schoolchildren, the audience for self-help books and TED Talks belong to the professional class. (Duckworth's *Grit,* along with Paul Tough's 2012 *How Children Succeed: Grit, Curiosity, and the Hidden Power of Character*) have spawned a small library of imitators.) Comfortable readers learn from such **leadership** books that their success is a deserved and just consequence of hard work in a fair system. Grit literature also reassures the desperate and frustrated that their situation is still within their control: a few tweaks or a new attitude are all you need to triumph in a job you love. One can imagine, however, how the payoff of such a philosophy could be pointless when it is not cruel. If parents "lay the foundation for grit," as Duckworth urges them to do, then a successful, determined, passionate child will grow up to confirm you did a good job; an unsuccessful, gritless child will simply make you blame yourself for her failures.[6] In neither case is there anything different you could now do about it. In other words, grit offers an explanation for what exists rather than giving us the tools to imagine something different.

What is ultimately most impressive about the literature of grit is the amount of intellectual energy expended in avoiding the obviously central fact of the economy. "Poverty" comes up a lot in Duckworth's book, but only as a condition, almost like the weather—one can only avoid it, not transform or eliminate it. Duckworth limits her discussion of the structural constraints on finding passion in work to a rather banal concession that yes, "there are very real constraints in the choices we can make about how we earn a living." At one point, she observes that "grit" can help people "defy the odds," a common enough vernacular turn of phrase for overcoming obstacles. Nevertheless, it's a surprising one for a social scientist to use, since defying the odds is, by definition, improbable.[7] And while it may work as advice in a business world predicated on competition, to fashion a democratic education policy around the possibility of defying odds makes little sense. If everyone, or even many people, could defy the odds, then casinos would be bankrupt.

This sublimated zest for hierarchy is the fundamental problem with grit, whether it is preached to poor children, wealthy ones, the unemployed, or the VP of sales. Like so many other familiar locutions used in American society to discuss class—"getting ahead," "climbing the ladder of opportunity," "social mobility"—grit is predicated, unspokenly but unmistakably, on the permanence of inequality. There must always be a bottom step on the "ladder of opportunity," after all. So, in order to succeed, be grittier than the next kid, defeat the listless and the unenthusiastic. For this reason, even as grit is dispatched for the children of the poor, you'll find its real audience perched atop the upper levels of our proverbial ladder.

HACK (N., V.); HACKER (N.)

The network hack is associated now with computers, but its meaning originates with the telephone. The first hacks invaded telephone switchboards and from there, the word expanded to other kinds of communication networks. The MIT Tech Model Railroad Club (TMRC), widely credited with coining the technophilic meaning of the noun "hack," defined it in its 1959 dictionary as "something done without constructive end." For the TMRC, a hack had much in common with a "prank," a faintly rebellious but not malicious demonstration of curiosity and mechanical ingenuity. The widespread accusation that the Russian government "hacked" the 2016 US presidential election relies on a newer meaning of the verb, as a subversive act of surveillance and manipulation. Meanwhile, in her book *Lifehacker: 88 Tech Tricks to Turbocharge Your Day*, Gina Trapani describes hacking as more benign than cybersurveillance and more constructive than the MIT club's original meaning, but deriving, like both, from the sense of an ingenious manipulation of technology. Borrowing a computing term, the "workaround," Trapani writes that a "lifehacker" "uses workarounds and shortcuts to overcome everyday difficulties of the modern worker."[1]

As these examples show, the meaning of "hack" tends to vacillate between two poles: either malice or mischief, subversion or collaboration, the dark side, or the light, the "black hat" or the "white hat," as Ben Yagoda writes.[2] This duality was apparent in one of the first investigations of hacking to appear in the

New York Times in August 1983. In a lengthy interview, Geoffrey Goodfellow, a computer security researcher in what was then a little town called Menlo Park, CA, described the hacker this way:

> A hacker is someone who programs computers for the sheer fun of it rather than, say, just theorizing about programming. A hacker could be described as a person capable of appreciating the irony and beauty—or as we refer to it, the "hack value"—of a program. But another part, unfortunately, is a little bit on the dark side. There is a malicious or inquisitive hacker, or meddler, who would like to discover information by poking around.

The article was illustrated by a grinning, masked cat burglar, cracking a computer depicted as a safe, a comically incongruous depiction of hacking's high-tech complexity, which was (and is) so unfamiliar to most people. The verb's most widespread current meanings still include Goodfellow's broad range: to hack is to covertly access a complex technological network in order to manipulate it for some end unintended by its designer or owner. This objective may be criminal, merely mischievous, politically subversive, or helpful —that is, it could improve the network in some way. For office workers bound by the computer, part of hacking's double meaning lies in its power to maximize productivity. Danny O'Brien, the tech writer who coined the term "lifehack," described it even more grandly as a form of self-realization, through which he "resolved to adapt the habits of the world's most organized and prolific geeks and become a Charles Atlas of organization."[3]

Hacking's link to "geeks" and computing betrays the technophilia of its MIT genealogy, but the common technological meaning derives from the word's sense of invasion. Hacking in the subversive sense operates via the manipulation and exposure of the informational networks by which, according to such hackers, we are misled, dominated, and betrayed. The actual political views of members of so-called hacktivist organizations like Anonymous can range widely: acting under the ethic of "transparency" and information freedom can motivate Chelsea Manning, who leaked classified US government material to WikiLeaks, telling a confidant that "information should be free," just as it (supposedly) motivated weev, the white supremacist hacker who once claimed to be "taking back the freedoms our forefathers assured us through technology" when he was sentenced for publicizing an AT&T security breach. Hacking in the activist sense often goes right along with "leaking"—hence the name WikiLeaks. Both terms can be read as the liberation of information held captive by bureaucracies that profit from their ownership of it; what one does with the information thus liberated, however, is the political question.[4]

A cyberphobic political meaning of "hacking" has become especially prominent in the controversy over the Russian government's interference in the 2016 US presidential election, which is often shorthanded in media reports as the "hacking" of the election. To "hack" an election is to cheat, to colonize with technological deceit a process that we like to imagine is driven by fair dealing and deliberation. The actual accomplishments of the Russian "hackers" are usually obscured by the paranoia attached to the shadowy, little-understood, seemingly sinister figure of the "hacker." "The Russians' efforts tend to be framed as a kind of giant machine," writes the journalist Adrian Chen. "The machine, we are told, is so sophisticated that only an expert, well-versed in terms such as 'exposure,' 'feedback loops,' and 'active measures,' can peer into the black box and explain to the layperson how it works." Fredric Jameson called this fixation on the "machine" of digital surveillance the "hysterical sublime." By this phrase Jameson refers to a generally hapless, paranoid attempt to make sense of the computing technologies of our time. The steam engines, turbines, or great factories of an earlier machine age could be painted, photographed, and filmed in a way that provoked terror, awe, and exhilaration, but in ways that also lent themselves to coherence and intelligibility. By contrast, the microchips and digital networks of our age cannot easily be understood or represented; they are not a single, discrete, giant "machine." Moreover, while we know these machines control our lives, few of us can begin to explain how they do it, what they look like, or who or what controls them.

The unrepresentability of the working mechanisms of computing networks is captured best by the "hacker" photos produced by stock photo agencies used to cheaply illustrate articles on identity theft and cybersecurity. Years after that first *New York Times* illustration of the hacker-as-safecracker, our representations of hackers trade in very old visual clichés borrowed from detective stories and pirate lore. In many examples, digital invisibility is represented by a mask and the hacker sits at a laptop equipped with quaint, old metonyms for burglary, like the thief's mask and the pirate's eye-patch, armed with weapons like guns and crowbars, which are comically irrelevant to the work at had. As Jameson writes, the hysterical sublime is a camp aesthetic.[5] Even if this stock-photo Hamburglar doesn't depict what a hacker actually does, the image does capture what almost all of us know and fear about the hacker—nothing and a lot, respectively. The "technology of contemporary society," writes Jameson, "is mesmerizing and fascinating . . . because it seems to offer some privileged representational shorthand for grasping a network of power and control even more difficult for our minds and imaginations to grasp." The ineptitude of the hacker stock photo tells us more than we might like to think about our own hapless, powerless, relationship to the decentered, digital world of capitalist computing technology. This is why hackers mobilize such anxiety. By methods we do not understand and cannot see, they threaten to take our identities and compromise our institutions, surveil our private thoughts and hijack our intimate moments; they are masked and faceless themselves, a sign of the fear that in encountering the internet "machine," we become disembodied ourselves.

Even as the cyberphobic figure of the foreign hacker occupies American headlines, a technophilic version of the hack also continues to thrive as a tool to improve the productivity of workers and the various machines they use. As critics like Nikil

Saval have observed, lifehacking, in spite of its cyberphilic air of novelty, owes a lot to Frederick Winslow Taylor, the nineteenth-century father of scientific management. Taylor set out to replace the "rule of thumb," in which workers worked at their own pace and by traditional standards, with more regularized, rationalized methods that would maximize their effort and minimize their cost in wages. "The management must take over and perform much of the work which is now left to the men; almost every act of the workman should be preceded by one or more preparatory acts of the management which enable him to do his work better and quicker than he otherwise could," he wrote in *The Principles of Scientific Management*. By contrast, the appeal of "lifehacking" is that it is self-directed—it is the kind of efficiency precisely "left to the men." But this sense of self-direction was also the goal of Taylor's system: "Each man should daily be taught by and receive the most friendly help from those who are over him, instead of being, at the one extreme, driven or coerced by his bosses, and at the other left to his own unaided devices," he wrote. Unless the worker internalizes scientific management, it would just engender more resentment and more shirking.[6]

"Lifehacking" does retain some of the hack's subversive meaning, since Trapani presents it as a form of resistance to overwork and surveillance in the white-collar office. Rather than resistance, though, what the lifehack offers is accommodation. It is a creature of white-collar employment; in the service sector, where workers have even less control over their time, "lifehacks" wouldn't fly. Hacking the scheduling software that traps retail or food service workers in at-will, part-time, so-called **flexible** work would just get you fired. But why call it "lifehacking" at all? Why not call it "work-hacking"? As the *Lifehacker* blog shows, one reason is that the verb "to hack" has expanded to all forms of non-working life. Leisure, travel, sleeping, children: virtually anything can be "hacked." Like the phrase "work-life balance," which subsumes one's "life" within "work" while presuming to separate them, the lifehack is another way in which the demands of ceaseless productivity penetrate our daily, non-working lives.

In an interview, Danny O'Brien describes the concept's appeal in a revealing way:

> [T]he idea of life hacks is just really appealing to geeks, because it's an expression of this huge hope that you can actually hack life in this way, that you might make it a bit more bearable without having to swallow or understand the whole thing.[7]

One expects that there is a "But . . ." coming at the end of this paragraph, but none arrives. O'Brien's vision of the hack is solidly on the bright side of the word's double meaning. Lifehacks articulate the "huge hope" that the problems of contemporary capitalist life are, contrary to appearances, actually bearable.

HUMAN CAPITAL (N.)

There is no entry in this book for "labor." This is because when people who speak the language of late capitalism want to refer to it, they say "human capital." "Investing in human capital" is a tried-and-true phrase favored by financial institutions, policy-wonks in mainstream US politics, and the global elites at the World Economic Forum in Davos, Switzerland. The Forum issues an annual "Global Human Capital Report," which in its most recent version was punctuated by pronouncements like "the world has developed only 62 percent of its human capital." The phrase has even entered the vocabulary of organized labor: after voting to strike, one Las Vegas casino worker denounced automation by saying, "The company needs to invest in human capital and treat us with dignity."[8]

And yet "human capital" was once controversial, precisely because the term connoted the opposite of "dignity." When the University of Chicago economist Theodore Schultz began developing his theory of human capital, it was haunted by the phrase's evocation of slavery. In his 1961 article "Investment in Human Capital," Schultz began by gingerly addressing the concept's potentially "offensive" sound. "Our values and beliefs inhibit us from looking upon human beings as capital goods, except in slavery, and this we abhor," he wrote. Any resemblance to human exploitation was purely coincidental, then, since human capital, far from reducing mankind to material, actually offered us the means of freedom. In 1962, at the height of the Cold War's ideological battle over the means to economic **freedom**, Schultz wrote that "by investing in themselves, people can enlarge the range of **choice** available to them. It is one way free men can enhance their welfare." Workers do this, he argued, by becoming capitalists themselves—not by acquiring property or stock, but by amassing knowledge and skills that have economic value. And their welfare, according to Schultz, could be enhanced by public policies geared toward improving their human capital. Schultz argued that a policy approach to human capital development would alleviate the social inequality of "many Negroes, Puerto Ricans, Mexican nationals, indigenous migratory farm workers, poor farm people and some of our older workers," and that their situation was a consequence of "our failure to have invested in their health and education." An appreciation of human capital and increased social investments in it, was to be a way of righting the wrongs seeded by previous uses of humans as capital.[9]

Gary Becker, Schultz's University of Chicago colleague, refined the human capital concept a decade later as the investments one makes—or, in increasingly rare cases, which one's employer or government makes—in individuals' knowledge, skills, health, and habits, all of the characteristics that shape their value in the labor market.[10] This is often how the term is now used in the positive sense of "talent"—as a kind of catchall term for labor, education, and health. For example, when the US Department of Education titles a section of its website "Improving Human Capital," it refers to labor policies in public schools—class sizes, layoff policies, and teacher pay—as well as teachers' education and pedagogical training. When Barack Obama spoke as president about supporting African **entrepreneurs** as a means of economic development on the continent, he used "human capital" to describe the education of an African workforce, but also to frame this project as African-led. The sense of a worker's agency that accrues to human capital by those who use the term sincerely is a product of Schultz and Becker's usage and their effort with it to reimagine labor apart from exploitation.[11]

The ideology of human capital is one source of the moral content of so many of the keywords in this book (even though capitalist moralism, like bourgeois evasions of "labor," go back a long way). When kindergarteners are chastened to master **grit** to enhance their college readiness, for example, this is the logic of human capital. **Creativity, flexibility, nimbleness**—these are personal, intangible "values" that can be said to enhance your "value" to your employer. The pressure to find **passion** at work is also an example of human capital's language of values, passion being an example of what Becker calls "psychic income"—the non-remunerative satisfactions one gets from work, presumably to supplement an unsatisfying regular income. The appeal of the term—ironically, given the way it once awkwardly summoned slavery to many who heard it—is that it is so seemingly neutral. When inequality is understood in the terms of human capital deficit, redressing those inequalities becomes not a matter of wealth redistribution, but human capital development (one can see examples of its influence in the popular liberal prescription of "job training" as a salve for unemployment). Another advantage to employers of treating education or health care as human capital development is that risk in labor markets can be outsourced to employees. Why train someone on the job when they might just leave and take their knowledge elsewhere? Why spend time and money teaching skills that may prove obsolete sooner than you think? And why pay into the health insurance of workers who insist on eating too much junk food on the weekend? Instead, let employees pay for their own college credentials and pursue their own **wellness** plan. The ideology of human capital asks one to think of nearly every form of social existence in terms of an actuarial calculation.

Yet human capital is usually described by business writers in terms of compassion, recognition, and appreciation. The most valuable asset of any company, it is often said, is its human capital. In other words, its people. In yet other words, its workers. "While it's completely obvious companies are built and run by humans," says one investor in *Forbes,* "it's not always obvious they are treated as valuable capital." The sympathetic mien of "human capital" is one reason, perhaps, that it is so often applied to global development, especially in Africa, the source of much of the Anglo-American world's current reserves of philanthropic sanctimony. For example, when the World Bank advertised a recent event on third-world development, "Building Human Capital: A Project for the World," it promoted it under the hashtag #investinpeople. The program's title evokes altruism rather than profit.

"Human capital," in our time, has therefore lost the ring of slavery that once worried Schultz. As Lester Spence observes, the human capital concept's reliance on our freedom is the source of its current power—it makes exhausting, costly obligations into an independently taken choice.[12] The ideology of human capital turns the toil we do for our bosses into something we do for our future selves, and the work we do for ourselves into something we do for our future bosses. As for human capital *as a concept,* though? It's mostly a specious synonym for "labor." As the Marxist economists Samuel Bowles and Herbert Gintis concluded pithily in a 1975 critique of the then-novel term, human capital doesn't mean much on its own terms, but it does make "a good ideology for the defense of the status quo."[13]

INNOVATION (N.)

For most of its early life, the word "innovation" was a pejorative, used to denounce false prophets and political dissidents. Thomas Hobbes used innovator in the seventeenth century as a synonym for a vain conspirator; Edmund Burke decried the innovators of revolutionary Paris as wreckers and miscreants; in 1837, a Catholic priest in Vermont devoted 320 pages to denouncing "the Innovator," an archetypal heretic he summarized as an "infidel and a sceptick at heart." The innovator's skepticism was a destructive conspiracy against the established order, whether in heaven or on earth. And if the innovator styled himself a seer, he was a false prophet. By the turn of the last century, though, the practice of innovation had begun to shed these associations with plotting and heresy. A milestone may have been achieved around 1914, when Vernon Castle, America's foremost dance instructor, invented a "decent," simplified American version of the Argentine tango and named it "the Innovation." "We are now in a state of transmission to more beautiful dancing," said Mamie Fish, the famed New York socialite credited with naming the dance. She told the *Omaha Bee* in 1914 that "this latest is a remarkably pretty dance, lacking in all the eccentricities and abandon of the 'tango,' and it is not at all difficult to do." No longer a deviant sin, innovation—and "The Innovation"—had become positively decent.[1]

The contemporary ubiquity of innovation is an example of how the world of business, despite its claims of rationality and empirical precision, also summons its own enigmatic mythologies. Many of the words in this volume orbit this one, deriving their own authority from their connection to the power of innovation. The value of innovation is so widespread and so seemingly self-evident that questioning it might seem bizarre—like criticizing beauty, science, or penicillin, things that are, like innovation, treated as either abstract human values or socially useful things we can scarcely imagine doing without. And certainly, many things called innovations are, in fact, innovative in the strict sense: original processes or products that satisfy some human need. A scholar can uncover archival evidence that transforms how we understand the meaning of a historical event; an automotive engineer can develop new industrial processes to make a car lighter; a corporate executive can extract additional value from his employees by automating production. These are all new ways of doing something, but they are very different somethings. Some require a combination of dogged persistence and interpretive imagination; others make use of mathematical and technical expertise; others, organizational vision and practical ruthlessness. But innovation as it is used most often today comes with an implied sense of benevolence; we rarely talk of innovative credit-default swaps or innovative chemical weapons, but innovations they plainly are. The destructive skepticism of the false-prophet innovator has been redeemed as the profit-making insight of the technological visionary.

Innovation is most popular today as a stand-alone concept, a kind of managerial spirit that permeates nearly every institutional setting, from nonprofits and newspapers to schools and children's toys. The *OED* defines innovation as "the alteration of what is established by the introduction of new elements or forms." The earliest example the dictionary gives dates from the mid-sixteenth century; the adjectival "innovative," meanwhile, was virtually unknown before the 1960s, but has exploded in popularity since. The verb "to innovate" has also seen a resurgence in recent years. The verb's intransitive meaning is "to bring in or introduce novelties; to make changes *in* something estab-

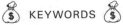

lished; to introduce innovations." Its earlier transitive meaning, "To change (a thing) into something new; to alter; to renew" is considered obsolete by the *OED*, but this meaning has seen something of a revival. This was the active meaning associated with conspirators and heretics, who were innovating the word of God or innovating government, in the sense of undermining or overthrowing each.

The major conflict in innovation's history is that between its formerly prohibited, religious connotation and the salutary, practical meaning that predominates now. Benoît Godin has shown that innovation was recuperated as a secular concept in the late nineteenth century and into the twentieth, when it became a form of worldly praxis rather than theological reflection. Its grammar evolved along with this meaning. Instead of a discrete irruption in an established order, innovation as a mass noun became a visionary faculty that individuals could nurture and develop in practical ways in the world; it was also the *process* of applying this faculty (e.g., "Lenovo's pursuit of innovation"). Innovation as a count noun—that is, *an* innovation—was in turn the product of this process (e.g., "the new iPhone features innovations like a high-resolution camera.") But this new meaning evolved slowly. The concept's old link to deceit and conspiracy shadowed its meaning into the twentieth century.[2]

Joseph Schumpeter, who elaborated an influential theory of innovation three years before the debut of the Innovation tango in his 1911 book *The Theory of Economic Development*, treated it as both a process and a product, with no sense of the old conspiratorial connotation. Schumpeter used "innovation" to describe capitalism's tendency toward tumult and transformation. Critical to his definition is the distinction Schumpeter makes between innovation as the refinement of a process or product, and invention, the creation of something entirely new. While Schumpeter was suspicious of the mythology of the inventor, the innovator, a more complex figure, was fundamental to the process he was describing. He understood innovation historically, as a process of economic transformation, but for him this historical process relied upon a creative, private agent to carry it out. Schumpeter's term for this agent was "the **entrepreneur**." To innovate, Schumpeter wrote later, was to "revolutionize the pattern of production by exploiting an invention or, more generally, an untried technological possibility for producing a new commodity." In the second decade of the twentieth century, the word began to appear regularly in **brand** names and advertisements (and short-lived dance crazes) in its now familiar form: as a new, improved product or process. One of the first major products to be advertised as an innovation was the Innovation wardrobe trunk, which Gimbel's department store offered in 1915 to appeal to customers' desires for the chimera of the new. (The trunks, the innovative features of which seem to have been their durability and "roomy construction," were so popular that an "innovation trunk" became a generic name for any trunk, like "Kleenex" is for tissues.)[3]

Although innovation has been thoroughly rehabilitated and purged of subversion, it retains its old accent of individual prophetic vision, the talent of those who, as Hobbes said of "innovators" in 1651, "suppose themselves wiser than others."[4] It is not that innovation has lost its old moral connotation; instead, it has reversed. What we once regarded as deviant and deceitful is now praised as visionary. In a 2011 reflection on the late Apple computer executive Steve Jobs, probably the archetypal hero-innovator of our time, a *San Francisco Chronicle* author praised his "constant desire to innovate and take chances." Here, the verb is used intransitively, in the more modern sense—that is, there is no direct object—but it lacks even the faintest hint of a reference. Jobs is no longer innovating *on* or *upon* anything in particular, which can make "innovate" sound like a kind of mantra. "If you don't innovate every day and have a great understanding of your customers," a Denver processed cheese executive told the *Denver Post* in 2010, "then you don't grow." And when the author of a *Wall Street Journal* obituary for Jobs writes that the Apple executive was a "secular prophet" who made innovation "a perfectly secular form of hope," it is apparent that the term has never really lost its old association with prophecy.[5]

Other than mystifying **creativity** itself—which now looks more like an intuitive blast of inspiration, like an epiphany, and less like work—"innovation" gives creativity a specific professional, class dimension. It is almost always applied to white-collar and profit-seeking activities, although its increasing popularity in educational contexts only reflects the creeping influence of **market**-based models in this field. Quality organizations are supposed to cultivate it in their employees by giving them the freedom to work independently and creatively. Rarely do we hear of the innovative carpenter, plumber, or homemaker, in spite of the imagination, improvisation, and managerial skills required of each. Business publications issue rankings of the "most innovative countries in the world," a curious usage that describes a) a capacity *constrained* by national borders, as if creativity dissipates or increases when one leaves passport control; and at the same time b) an intrinsic human talent unconstrained by fields, industries, or media. Another example of the term's increasing mystification is the acceptability of the tautological construction "to innovate innovation." "Who's the Best at Innovating Innovation?" asks the *Harvard Business Review*; the same publication sponsors a lucrative prize called the "Innovating Innovation Challenge." One can "innovate" without having to act upon any process or idea other than the act of innovation itself. One simply innovates in circles, forever. Innovation is an example of the ways in which (as we can see with the rise of **content**) the production and circulation of commodities becomes imbued with fantastic and even theological properties detached from the labor that produces them, or in the case of many common uses of the verb "to innovate," detached from any object.[6] So when liberal politicians promote an "innovation agenda" that includes student debt forgiveness for "startup founders," as Hillary Clinton did during her 2016 presidential campaign, it is unclear how this differs from any other form of corporate welfare. And when conservative politicians or CEOs lament how labor unions or public regulation of the private sector "impede innovation," we can recognize this as both a ludicrous obfuscation but also another example of the bourgeois contempt for labor.[7]

Innovation is thus a theological concept which became a theory of commodity production and which has lately become a commodity itself. The innovator, meanwhile, has always been identified with novelty and visionary charisma. But where the innovator's visions were once widely feared as venal and destructive, now innovation is understood as the refinement of a technical process, in which creativity is turned to profit. But as the mythic figure of Jobs makes clear, rather than replacing prophecy with procedure, modern celebrations of innovation supplement each with the other. From the business world to education and politics, innovation is simultaneously spiritual and technological, both an individual's reaction against bureaucratic malaise and the spirit of anti-orthodox creativity to be cultivated by the same bureaucracy.[8] Innovation, therefore, is a strangely contradictory concept, simultaneously grandiose and modest, saccharine and pessimistic. The prophetic meaning embedded deep in its history allows innovation to stand in for nearly any kind of positive transformation, doing for the twenty-first century what "progress" once did for the nineteenth and twentieth. In the United States, innovation also suggests a high-tech update to the myth of "Yankee ingenuity" or "know-how"—the spirit of mechanical cleverness and entrepreneurial energy once associated with New England's **artisan** class.[9] Like the mythical inventors of the American industrial age—Alexander Graham Bell and Thomas Edison tinkering in their workshops—the innovator is a model capitalist citizen for our times. But the object of most innovations today is more elusive: you can touch a telephone or a phonograph, but who can lay hands on an Amazon algorithm, a credit-default swap, a piece of proprietary Uber code, or an international free trade agreement? As an intangible, individualistic, yet strictly white-collar trait, innovation reframes the cruel fortunes of an unequal global economy as the logical products of a creative, visionary brilliance. In this new guise, the innovator retains both a touch of the prophet and a hint of the confidence man.

LEADERSHIP (N.)

Every gangster, stock trader, and aspiring tough-guy's favorite strategy manual, Sun Tzu's *The Art of War*, counsels humility and generosity as the essence of leadership. "A good commander is benevolent, and unconcerned with fame." Another expert sounds a similar note: "The leader's first task is to be the trumpet that sounds a clear sound." Another argues that good leaders

> create a vision, articulate the vision, passionately own the vision, and relentlessly drive it to completion. Above all else, though, good leaders are open. They go up, down, and around their organization to reach people. They don't stick to the established channels.

Are leaders born or made, asked the same author in another interview? (Unsurprising answer: both.) A fourth insisted that leaders must be "modest and prudent and guard against arrogance and impetuosity; they must be imbued with the spirit of self-criticism and have the courage to correct mistakes and shortcomings in their work."[1]

The first bromide comes from Paulie Walnuts, the dutiful soldier in Tony Soprano's crew on *The Sopranos*, paraphrasing his boss's quotation of "Sun tuh-zoo, the Chinese Prince Machiavelli." The principle of clarity and candor comes from Peter Drucker, a preeminent figure in management studies, whose work emphasized qualitative "values" and emotional intelligence instead of quantitative facility and efficiency. The next piece of advice, on creating, articulating, and owning the vision, comes from Jack Welch, the former chairman of GE. The fourth principle, of humility and self-criticism, comes from Mao Tse-Tung's *Little Red Book,* on the training of "cadres," the French-derived word used in Communist parties to describe local party leaders.

These examples rehearse some common themes in the vast literature on that impossibly broad abstraction, "leadership." First is the leadership writer's mania for quotation, which is to say, a mania for authority: in his reverence for both Sun Tzu (or an approximation of him) Paulie stands in the company of many business writers who reverently pepper their manuals with inspiring quotations mined from anyone from Thoreau to Emerson to Galileo, historical context be damned. The second routine feature of leadership advice is how routinely it contradicts itself. A leader is decisive and commanding, but also humble and open; he owns the vision, but also delegates it; he is a trumpet, but also a listener; he is results-oriented, and he is a visionary; he is independent-minded but devoted to the authority of quotable eminences. One consistency: he is usually a man. The literature of leadership celebrates gendered notions of decisiveness and authority, but much of it is also "spiritual" in the broad, New Age sense of that word: that is, oriented toward the self and to esoteric matters of character. And as the popularity of the "guru" concept makes clear, much of this spiritualist aspect of leadership literature reveals a prominent thread of Orientalism, which trades upon an idiosyncratic, esoteric wisdom associated stereotypically with Asian men of a certain age. That even Mao has been recuperated as a management guru—in the *Economist,* no less—underscores this point. One cannot imagine seeing, say, Stalin's *Mastering Bolshevism* excerpted in *Entrepreneur* magazine, although I have read enough of this literature to also say that you really never know.[2]

We are drowning in leadership, from presidential politics and business literature to schooling and child-rearing.[3] An ideal of "decisive leadership" has long been invoked by preening political candidates presenting themselves as steely-eyed generals staring down ISIS, unemployment, or a sluggish stock market.

The leader fetish reached a recent zenith with Donald Trump's presidential campaign. In Trump, who sought the presidency in a period of crisis and then claimed that he alone could fix it, an ostensibly democratic populace once again embraced a faith in charismatic leadership. Leadership is the bread and butter of Harvard Business Publishing, *Harvard Business Review*'s book publishing wing, where it is by far the most prolific subject area. Undergraduate majors and PhD programs increasingly teach the subject, and college admissions counselors demand it of successful applicants.[4] At the University of Illinois's Leadership Center— trademarked, unlike most academic programs—students can take classes on "Food and Agribusiness Management," "Strategies of Persuasion," or "The US Presidency." The Center's mission statement begins with a celebratory epigraph that might be better taken as a warning: "Leadership is the most observed, yet least understood, phenomena on earth." The statement trundles bravely forward: "Leaders are individuals who work with others to create positive change," and "leadership can be practiced by anyone interested in making a contribution, regardless of formal authority or position." Here is the central paradox of leadership, and indeed of the self-help literature that has lately popularized the concept: on the one hand, there is a reverence for authority intrinsic to the meaning of the word. On the other hand, many treatments of leadership define it with Illinois's vague, can-do populism: everyone can and should be a leader, whether they are in charge or not. Statements like Illinois's seem to use "leadership" where institutions might have once used more democratic values like "citizenship," which suggests that the reason we don't yet understand leadership isn't that the concept is too complex— it's that it's too shallow.

This paradox of authority and populism is nothing new either. How-to-be-rich authors and leadership sages who style themselves as Welch-like visionaries might be disappointed to learn that many of their ideas also recapitulate older ones: what Joshua Rothman calls the "trait model" of leadership is one example. Welch and Steve Jobs have been often cited for their strengths of personality and character. Illinois's leadership curriculum includes a privately-owned personality test called the Clifton StrengthsFinder, developed by the psychologist and self-help author Don Clifton, which purports to find the test-takers' personal talents. Nineteenth-century leadership "gurus" did not offer to find your latent leadership traits; instead, they offered portraits of "men of industry" whose admirable traits could be imitated. But these leaders also had an alluring ordinariness that made their traits imitable, just as leadership can now be found far from the C-suite. For example, in his 1885 book *Men of Invention and Industry,* Samuel Smiles devotes one chapter to a man named Francis Pettit Smith who grew rich after perfecting a screw propeller for steamships. But Smith, clever as he was, "was not a great inventor," wrote Smiles. Instead, what he had was "determined tenacity" to apply an invention made by others.[5]

Late twentieth- and twenty-first century celebrants of leadership have softened the heroic, conventionally masculine leadership traits of decisiveness and firmness with a feminized language of self-reflection and aesthetics that derived, in part, from the same workplace psychology that wrought **creativity** and the self-actualized employee.[6] This, too, has a long history, however: in his 1936 bestseller *How to Win Friends and Influence People,* Dale Carnegie emphasized the value of empathy in building "influence." Using the rather odd analogy of dogs and babies—who are both interested in other people without ulterior motive, he claims—Carnegie urged his readers to practice, or at least perform, the characteristic of selfless curiosity. (One doubts how much time Carnegie really spent with human babies.) As it goes with dogs and babies, so it goes with professional writers: in another anecdote, Carnegie reports a creative writing professor telling him that good writers must be interested in people. "If that is true of writing fiction," concludes Carnegie, "you can be sure it is true of dealing with people face to face."[7] Leadership has long been understood in such terms, as less an innate trait of decisiveness and more of a teachable "art" of reading and managing people. Norman Vincent Peale's 1952 self-help classic

The Power of Positive Thinking was itself an heir to an even earlier introspective tradition in American self-help literature. The late nineteenth-century New Thought or mind-cure movement "emphasized the individual's power to achieve well-being and prosperity through positive visualization," writes Beth Blum, a scholar of self-help's literary history. Mind-cure advocates shared with their contemporary leadership descendants an investment in cultivating innate traits and an interest in "Eastern" religion. As Blum notes, Wallace Wattles, the mind-cure proponent and author of the 1910 best seller, *The Science of Getting Rich*, claimed Hindu monistic theory as an inspiration. He was not yet called a leadership "guru," however; that particular **innovation** would come later.[8]

One thing we can conclude from all of the above is that like many other corporate keywords in this volume, leadership means very little, but it offers quite a lot. What it offers is a sense of control and a sense of justice. To underpaid subordinates lost in bureaucracies, the populist model of leadership offers a sense of agency, the possibility of advancement and appreciation. Leadership courses taken by those already born on third base, meanwhile, might offer the comforting confirmation that they deserve their advantage. And for those who are already in charge, the fetish for leadership only enhances their value. The rewards of leadership come into clearer focus when we compare it to words it replaces—"management," for example. Williams notes how "management," as a private "body of paid agents to administer increasingly large business concerns," came in English to be distinguished from "the bureaucracy" or "the administration," words associated with the state and other public institutions. As the distinction between public and private business seems to wither, a single word, "leadership," is coming to replace the terms that once marked public administration as something distinct from profit-driven business. It is harder than ever to tell, for example, how running a government "like a business" is distinct from running it for personal profit, or how most universities' nonprofit "administration" differs markedly from their private, for-profit "management."[9] Leadership bridges these dwindling divides.

"Leader" has another synonym, of course: "boss," which implies a relation based on coercion and exploitation. Leadership instead summons a host of abstractions about personal character, which is why so many doctrines of leadership sometimes read like prayers, with their allusive, circular abstraction, their air of authority and ancient wisdom, and their reliance on a roster of prophets—Sun Tzu, Emerson, or whomever. To borrow a phrase that Blum uses to describe the twentieth-century self-help literature from which it springs, leadership is "secularism with benefits." In its anxious repetitions, it borrows the sound of a mantra, and in its gestures to abstract principles and "Eastern" faiths, it approximates the depth and wisdom of liturgy, but always with the expectation of material reward: all the benefits of a faith without any of its harder demands—reckoning with doubt, for example. As Jack Welch says somewhere, doubt is not a leadership quality.[10]

LEAN (ADJ., N.)

Lean is the fountainhead from which much of the body-talk of austerity has sprung. The lean ideal of cost-cutting efficiency begat **nimble** and **flexible**, two other terms for workplaces trimmed of labor inefficiency. Lean production maximizes workers' effort, productivity, and according to its advocates, their emotional investment in their work, all while minimizing "waste." Like nimble, in which a company is metaphorically imagined as an athletic individual, lean imagines the firm as a disciplined, practiced body. It's lean, in other words, like a cut of meat, not lean as in "lean years." This distinction is important, as it foregrounds the question raised obliquely by the term "waste"—what, and most importantly who, becomes the waste in a lean economy?

"Lean production" was coined in 1988 by John Krafcik, who was a participant in an influential MIT study led by James Womack on the future of the automobile. The term was popularized in the influential 1991 book *The Machine That Changed the World*, co-authored by Womack. Lean production was Krafcik's term for the manufacturing philosophy otherwise known as the Toyota Production System, developed by the Japanese automaker to confront capital shortages in postwar Japan. *The Machine That Changed the World* begins with an illustrative example: in an auto plant, rolls of steel are cut or shaped by a die, which stamps the raw steel into necessary pieces. In conventional auto plants at the time, various specialized dies were maintained constantly, and the parts they produced were stockpiled for eventual assembly. Toyota, unable to afford the large number of production lines and warehouse facilities standard in other auto plants, devised a system in which its die makers could rotate various dies on a single production line quickly and deliver the resulting parts on demand, mitigating the need for multiple dies and an extensive stockpile of parts—and the workers to handle both. Toyota could produce cars with fewer defects with much less inventory on site, and do it more quickly, resulting in a greater variety of products that could be changed quickly in response to consumer demand. The Toyota Production System is often shorthanded as "just-in-time" production—for the rate at which supplies arrive at the plant before they are converted into a manufactured product. "Lean production," the authors write in *The Machine That Changed the World*, "is 'lean' because it uses less of everything compared with mass production—half the human effort in the factory, half the engineering hours to develop a new product in half the time."[11]

A critical part of lean production's practical method and its ideological power is its reliance on the idea of flexibility. Because a lean facility does not need to maintain a large inventory of parts, it can produce new products more quickly than a conventional factory. To make the most of a lean facility's assets, however, the plant must run longer, with more shifts. It must constantly seek new methods to maximize productivity at lower cost—what Toyota calls *kaisen,* or "constant improvement." Workers take on more individual responsibility, and broader job requirements for individual workers means greater efficiency in the production line and less "slack time," since in a lean facility there is always something that everyone must do. In order to extract the maximum value from its limited fixed capital, Toyota's production system also placed a premium on employees' identification with the company, organizing workplace authority around small "teams" and rewarding employee loyalty with material benefits like bonus payments tied to profitability. The **collaborative** team ideal represents the ideological thrust of flexibility in the lean workplace. Lean is "truly a system of reciprocal obligation," write Womack and his colleagues, overstating their case, given the fact that the plant manager does not reciprocate his salary. "Lean is a people-based system," goes an oft-repeated slogan in lean enterprise circles. It would be a mistake, however, to regard workplace teams as mere ideological window-dressing on the same old exploitation. The team model does rely on the initiative of workers in order to function properly; a system with such a slim margin for error requires at some level the solicitude of employees.[12] As one critic writes, "lean production makes a deliberate and explicit effort to organize the informal social network in the production system to align employee interests as closely as possible with company goals."[13] Workers in a lean facility owe obligations to one another, but these ties become entangled with the "Toyota family." By replacing the authoritarian rule of the foreman with the informal authority of one's workmates, workplace teams achieve labor flexibility in practical ways, like eliminating the need for "buffers," or utility workers kept on hand to compensate for the regular absenteeism in a mass production facility. Lean "pushes responsibility down the ladder," devolving decision-making responsibility to teams of workers while maximizing their productivity. Labor critics like Kim Moody, who see lean production as an intensified form of Taylorist scientific management rather than a substantially new mode of production, note that teams are still implementing directives that come, as ever, from management. They do so in a way that devolves not only authority but surveillance from

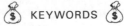

the bosses to the production line, eroding solidarity on the shop floor. A sluggish team member who had a beer at lunch now lets his whole group down. The scientific manager with a stopwatch and a clipboard becomes your fellow worker, rather than a loathed consultant from outside.[14]

Lean production has clear material benefits, but like the other bodily terms in the volume, it has a distinct moral resonance as well. Corporate leaders have often presumed to be philosophers, but "lean," the pursuit of "constant improvement" in all things, is almost metaphysical to the consultants and business writers who promote it. "Lean"—and it is often shorthanded in this way, like an ancient rite—is not just a faster way of producing fenders and axles. It "is not a tactic or a cost-reduction program," intones the Lean Enterprise Institute in its introduction to the concept, "but a way of thinking and acting for an entire organization."[15]

MAKER (N.)

What is a "maker"? *Make* magazine, the organ of what it calls the "Maker Movement," says that "tinkerers, educators, parents, and professionals are makers," but then again, "we are all Makers."[1] A maker is an **artisan** without the history of class consciousness; making is the countercultural ethos of **DIY,** minus the home repair; it is crafting with more technology and fewer women. While the artisan, crafter, and maker respond in some way to a suspicion of industrial capitalist methods and structures, making exhibits an enthusiastic embrace of technology. The maker/crafter distinction, moreover, betrays the gender inequality that infuses any discussion of the computing technology often shorthanded as "tech." Making is practical, futuristic, **innovative,** masculine, prestigious; crafting is ornamental, old-fashioned, traditional, feminized, quaint. Making breaks molds or fabricates new ones; crafting sews from a pattern.

The word "maker" is not often heard outside of the context of maker culture; the word is most often encountered affixed to something else, as in "candy-maker" or "watchmaker." But the noun "maker" is quite old—today's makers might have been called "makers-up" or "maker-uppers" in the nineteenth century. Then, the word corresponded roughly to "skilled worker," and was used often in the printing and textile trades. Today's noun "maker" appears as if it is meant as a neologistic back-formation from the transitive verb "to make." *Make* magazine, which claims to have coined the term in 2005, emphasizes the

action of making along with the identity of the maker, high-
lighting the verb and its attendant agency. Where most passively
buy, the idea seems to be, others dare to make. Making, its
founder says on the magazine's website, "is a meaningful form of
personal expression that fosters **creativity**, builds community and
encourages the **collaborative** practice of innovation." The slogan,
"We are all makers," sounds like a populist note that emphasizes
a sense of feisty purpose. Makers are unleashing their universal
human creativity, never merely working.

As Evgeny Morozov has written, the contemporary political
valence of "makers" (and their more mischievous confrères, the
hackers) has a history that draws upon various sources. One is the
defiant amateurism and community-mindedness of punk DIY
culture, with its handmade zines and home-recorded albums (a
genealogy suggested by *Make*'s URL, makezine.com). Another
is the 1960s Whole Earth catalog, which advocated simplifying
and cultivating the skills and technologies to bypass corporate
capitalism and is routinely cited now, by both critical historians and mythmakers of Silicon Valley, as a source of the industry's iconoclastic self-definition. Making is also a descendant
of the turn-of-the-century Arts and Crafts movement, which
reacted to the factory's conquest of the artisan by promoting and
preserving threatened craft production methods. In the United
States in particular, the maker as tinkerer, problem solver, and
autonomous creator draws on nineteenth-century myths of
Yankee "know-how," personified by the independent mechanic
or artisan. This complex inheritance gives makers a rebellious
posture and an establishment prestige. The "maker movement,"
writes Dale Dougherty, *Make*'s cofounder, "has come about in
part because of people's need to **engage passionately** with objects in ways that make them more than just consumers." On
the other hand, when the Obama White House hosted its own
"Maker Faire," it dispensed with the anti-consumerism talk and
promoted making as a way to encourage "maker **entrepreneurs**"
and "foster the development of advanced manufacturing in the

US." Other self-described makers have followed suit, embracing factory automation as the mainstream future of their movement.[2]

Unlike artisans, who celebrate antiquated production methods, makers tend not to criticize machines so much as celebrate unforeseen possibilities for them. It's an old utopian dream that social inequities and alienation under capitalism could be overcome, and the productive forces unleashed, by simplifying and distributing the technological tools to those who lack them. The belief in the benevolence of technological progress is captured by a word favored in the making, computing, and software industries for the technologies that they produce: "tools." A tool is neutral—a hammer can be used to build a house or break a finger. But the word's neutrality is something of a ruse and an alibi, a reason why tech-industry executives under duress routinely describe their products this way. There is something idealistic about "tools," given the word's implication of well-intentioned problem-solving.[3] Mark Twain satirized a nineteenth-century ancestor of the maker in *A Connecticut Yankee at King Arthur's Court*, his 1889 story of a Colt factory foreman who hit his head and woke up in Arthurian England. Hank Morgan was an archetypal Yankee tinkerer: "I could make anything a body wanted—anything in the world, it didn't make any difference what," Morgan says by way of introduction. "And if there wasn't any quick new-fangled way to make a thing, I could invent one—and do it as easy as rolling off a log." And he proves himself right, making telephones, advertising, laundry soap, and electricity in a quest to pull medieval Britons out of superstition and inefficiency. But the Yankee comes to find that he rather likes being named "Sir Boss," as his feudal underlings call him, and his modern technologies gradually come to serve as instruments of his own power. By the novel's famous ending, when Morgan massacres the knights who revolt against him by electrifying their armor, Yankee know-how has collapsed into electrified barbarism. 3-D printing may not lead us to such catastrophe, of course. But the olde English spelling of the Maker Faires should give every Twain reader pause. Every generation of Americans has its apolitical dream of liberation through technology, and the bulletproof confidence to match it.

MARKET, MARKETPLACE (N.)

The market is both a widely dispersed metaphor of exchange and an economic term often used as a shorthand for capitalist forms *of* exchange, especially when modified by the adjective "**free**." Even as an economic concept, however, the market and marketplace are often used metaphorically. It is striking that a concept so central to the political and economic discourse of the late twentieth and early twenty-first centuries is so promiscuously used and elusively defined.

The word's oldest meaning is its simplest: "a place at which trade is conducted," a meaning that appears in Old English as far back as the twelfth century. This spatial meaning of the market*place* obviously persists in farmer's markets, stock markets, and supermarkets, but today the market is also something more abstract. The most recent definition given by the *OED* is "the competitive free market; the operation of supply and demand." Its first example of this usage comes from 1970, at the rough beginning of a neoliberal era marked by financial deregulation and deindustrialization in the Global North and structural adjustment in the Global South.[4] The original sense of "the market" as a spatially and temporally bounded place to exchange goods continues to inform its most abstract and ideological uses. Even in highly technical and immaterial trades, like software development, it is still common to describe the launch of a product as "bringing it to market," as if it is ridden into town on an oxcart. And the idea of a competitive free market derives some of its presumed vitality from the street market: its frenetic activity and its self-regulating logic, in which prices adjust to whatever "the market will bear," in the common phrase. This last definition of the market is a fiction—not a lie, necessarily, but a story, in which the freedom of and in a market is a matter not of fact but of interpretation and perspective. As Slobodian points out, even critics of neoliberalism's exaltation of the market accept, implicitly, this presumption of vitality. As he writes, "the otherwise uncommon adjective 'unfettered' is attached habitually to 'markets' as both neoliberal goal and putative reality." When critics describe the "unfettered markets" unleashed by NAFTA, for example, they implicitly accept the idea that the market is, in fact, otherwise fettered, and that neoliberals' goal is actually to set it free. As Slobodian insists, though, even earnest neoliberals understand the market as "a set of relationships that rely on an institutional framework" that must be designed to serve capital, rather than a natural phenomenon yearning to breathe free. After all, that's why they negotiated NAFTA.[5]

A market is thus a fiction, a place, and a set of relationships. When you "corner a market," you assert control over "the arena in which commercial dealings in a particular commodity or product are conducted." Here again is the persistent spatial fiction of the *marketplace*: we are clearly not speaking of a literal "arena," but a medium of commodity exchange and a set of relationships between buyers, sellers, workers, and regulators. The market is also used as a metaphor for exchange in other, noneconomic contexts, like the "marketplace of ideas," the unmediated contest of ideas within institutions or societies, a sphere of unfettered competition in which merit prevails. The first use of the phrase "marketplace of ideas" in the *New York Times* came courtesy of the Communist Party USA, in an op-ed column outlining its political platform for the 1948 presidential elections. "We Communists seek only the opportunity to compete fairly in the marketplace of ideas," the party pleaded, defending their political legitimacy in the early Cold War. In the twenty-first century, American political rhetoric carries on this tradition of conflating the "free market" and democracy.[6]

The strangeness of the Communist Party inaugurating a metaphor for intellectual exchange based on a term for private commerce can be explained as a desperate political gambit. But what is remarkable about the market-democracy metaphor is its elision of an obvious fact of literal marketplaces: they are by definition unequal. Participation in markets is shaped by one's capital and mobility (both physical and, in the intellectual metaphor, communicational—that is, the mobility afforded one's ideas by the media, universities, or publishing houses one can access). And what is for sale in the marketplace of ideas? What is the currency? Who prevents the sale of tainted goods? As Marnie Holborow and David Graeber observe, these models of an intellectual "market" rely on a meaningless sense of value. One can assess the value of a can of coffee relative to a bottle of orange juice, and use money to quantify the difference. But to evaluate the meaning of ideas in a marketplace, one needs to measure their worth from some point of reference outside the marketplace—in other words, how can one judge ideas, unless they have ideas already?[7]

This fiction of the marketplace as self-regulating and naturally unfettered has shaped the popular discourse of free markets in political discussion since the 1970s. When politicians speak of "market forces" they presume their autonomy; we are creatures of the market, rather than the other way around. This assertion of naturalness produces certain paradoxes: the concept of "market failure" grapples with those curious realms of human experience resistant to its regulatory efficiencies, like health care or the warming earth itself, which is subject to the ecological market failure of mass extinction.[8] And one of the ways in which the market's autonomy is reiterated in popular media and economics discourse is a peculiar anthropomorphism of a market's psychology: "nervous" markets, markets that are "sullen," markets that react to political events "skittishly," as if the markets are frightened puppies in a thunderstorm, rather than the thunderstorm itself.[9] Although a nervous market would seem all too human, the paradoxical effect of such phrasing is to characterize the market as suprahuman and autonomous. Yet as Philip Mirowski describes it, for the neoliberal Austrian economist Friedrich Hayek, markets were neither nervous nor wise sorters of our fortunes; instead, the market was "an information processor" modeled on a mid-century telephone exchange. The market was neither natural nor autonomous, neither the absence of the state nor a primal condition of human society. Instead, it was a man-made network that required a strong state to enforce its domain. And in key moments of recent economic history—the United States government's Troubled Asset Relief Program, the European austerity measures to enforce "market discipline" on Greece— market autonomy is nowhere to be seen. Thus, the myth of the neoliberal market as autonomous and natural is just that, a myth. Neoliberalism is neither the unfettering of the market nor the retreat of the state.[10]

The gap between the market's literal and metaphorical meanings has yielded a basic confusion about a concept that is often presumed, rarely defined, and—because it so often functions as an ideal—whose very existence is questionable. A synonym for exchange, whether intellectual or economic, an ontological feature of human social life, an implacable natural force, or a cybernetic network reliant on a strong state: the market can be whatever you need it to be.

MERITOCRACY (N.)

Meritocracy is a recent coinage, whose original satirical political meaning has become so corrupted with use that it is now used earnestly to name the very idea—an elite caste made by talent and education—that its original use was meant to disparage. In 1958 British sociologist Michael Young coined the word in his book, *The Rise of the Meritocracy*, which describes a dystopian society in a future Britain when compulsory schooling and a competitive civil service has replaced the inherited privileges of class society. Young's coinage was a portmanteau of "merit" and "aristocracy," and his point wasn't that educational notions of merit were displacing the class-based distribution of privileges, but rather *replacing* them. In other words, if status is to be distributed through the "talents" nurtured in education, then access to education would become the new means of reproducing aristocratic status. "Today," writes Young from the imagined perspective of 2033, "we frankly recognize that democracy can be no more than aspiration, and have rule not so much by the people as by the cleverest people; not an aristocracy of birth, not a plutocracy of wealth, but a true meritocracy of talent."[11] As Young himself wrote in a 2001 essay deploring his term's enthusiastic adoption by the New Labour government of Tony Blair, that education had become a means of concentrating power. "It is good sense," he wrote, "to appoint individual people to jobs on their merit. It is the opposite when those who are judged to have merit of a particular kind harden into a new social class without room in it for others."[12] In short, Blair had missed the point of meritocracy, embracing the ideal of "merit" while forgetting the "aristocracy" part.

In the United States, which lacks the British class consciousness that informed Young's term, the concept of meritocracy has proliferated with little sense of its original satirical meaning. Some critics use the term skeptically, as an unkept promise of egalitarianism, which the common phrase "myth of meritocracy" captures. Chris Hayes argues that meritocracy exerts such a hypnotic pull precisely because of the way it sidelines uncomfortable discussions about class and other inherited privileges. America's meritocracy is a rhetorical point of consensus that "undergirds our debates," he writes, "but is itself never the subject of them." For Lauren Berlant, American meritocracy is a fantasy of "being deserving," a form of "cruel optimism" that sustains the belief that those who are cleverest and try hardest will surely be judged worthy—an ostensibly egalitarian sheen for a mean class system. Other affirmative uses of the term identify it with a kind of benevolent, technocratic efficiency. In Singapore, where meritocracy is an officially sanctioned national myth, the idea takes on an especially hierarchical cast that comes closer to approximating Young's original meaning. Tyler Cowen, a libertarian economist, rather gleefully images a future society (iWorld, he calls it, not trying very hard or very cleverly) organized by mastery of computing technology in his book *Average is Over*. He imagines a "hyper-meritocracy" of those able to keep up the pace of technological change and expertise. Cowen sums up this competitive meritocracy: "If you and your skills are a complement to the computer, your wage and labor prospects are likely to be cheery." "If your skills do not complement the computer, you may want to address that mismatch." A "meritocracy" like this seems less like the ideal society of egalitarian opportunity it has become, and more like the educated aristocracy it was originally intended to be.[13]

NIMBLE (ADJ.)

When large-scale faculty layoffs began at the University of Southern Maine in 2014, a philosophy professor named Jason Read wrote a detailed account of the assembly where the university president announced the cuts:

> Words like "metropolitan," "**innovative**," and "nimble" passed from the president of the university and the chancellor of the system to the members of the board of trustees, all from banking, corporate law, and the business sector, constituting a dismal display of the current corporate common sense. . . . The recasting of the university as corporation that must "adapt or die" was coupled with disparaging remarks about shared governance, union contracts, and public debates over the fate of a public university.

Layoffs are necessary to make a more nimble university, says the university president. What does nimble mean, and what is its opposite?[1]

Google's ngram database shows that "nimble" has remained steadily popular for the last two centuries. It was once a children's book staple, reflecting the word's literal meanings, which are applicable to instructive and vigorous play, as well as active brains and dexterous hands: "Quick at grasping, comprehending, or learning," according to the *OED,* and "light in movement or action."[2] The word literally refers to intellectual quickness or physical dexterity in an individual person, as in Jack's famous leap over the candlestick. Well into the 1980s, it appeared in the *New York Times* most often in the sports section. An early, rare business usage appeared in a 1981 headline, "Nimble Commodities Broker," above an article about the merger of two Wall Street commodities trading firms. (The author of that article: a young reporter named Thomas L. Friedman.) The adjective is also popular in literary criticism as a term of praise for the dynamism of a writer's prose style. Although one occasionally still sees it applied to dexterous athletes, nimble is now most often used in mainstream journalism in a business context, as a metaphorical synonym for "efficient." It was ubiquitous in media coverage of the General Motors and Chrysler bankruptcies of 2009, misfortunes commonly attributed to the companies' size and inefficiency. The layoffs of tens of thousands of employees were reforms necessary to make more nimble companies, it was said. Here, the word was plainly euphemistic, depicting the firm as an overweight body that needed to slim down and get in shape, rarely stating the human consequences of "nimbleness" outright. GM was "bloated" and a "behemoth," causing it, wrote a *New York Times* reporter, to "lose a step to more nimble competitors," especially Japanese automakers. (It is hard not to notice how this usage also plays on common American physical stereotypes of both blue-collar US midwesterners and Asians.)[3]

Like the related concepts of **lean** and **flexible,** nimble optimistically describes a sort of labor discipline, in which individual employees, in a variety of fields, assume more and more tasks once performed by separate employees. The University of Southern Maine's president was using the concept in this way, cushioning the blow by presenting layoffs as a hard but healthy decision. In a 2010 news report on layoffs in the journalism industry, nimble referred to the willingness of an employee to assume the labor and learn the skills once provided by another paid staffer. "They're going to have to be more nimble both journalistically and technically in terms of the production of their pieces," said a reporter of the additional work of writing and editing that the journalists who remain must do in the field.[4] A nimble organization, in short, maximizes productivity while minimizing labor

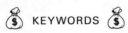

costs. Nimble is athletic, vigorous, youthful, and gymnastic, like the boy who jumps over the candlestick. Never mind that nimbleness is so often a vaporous concept. Much of the language of late capitalism imagines workplaces as bodies in virtually every way except as a group of overworked or underpaid ones.

OUTCOME (N.)

Outcome has two particularly relevant definitions that date to the latter half of the nineteenth century. One is "the product which results from an action, process, or system," and the other is "a state of affairs resulting from some process . . . a result (of a test, experiment, measurement, etc.)." It is, by itself, an innocent word. Every process produces results, and it is sensible to try to measure them. Health outcomes, to use one common example, are studied to assess how a patient or population responds to particular treatments. Policy outcomes describe the consequences of a government program. It is the outcome's link to products and measurement that gives it its place in this volume—particularly in my own field of education.

The pedagogical theory of "outcomes-based education" was originally part of a turn to "student-centered" learning in the 1990s. By emphasizing the product of a curriculum or lesson, the argument went, teachers could give students greater clarity in what they were expected to learn and adapt to students' needs more easily. But outcome-based education was also a response to the school-reform movement's demand for **accountability** in instruction, which emphasized uniform standards over local idiosyncrasy. Outcomes, therefore, could mean different things to different sorts of critics. Liberals approached outcomes as anti-authoritarian and student-centered; conservatives emphasized assessable educational standards, criticizing these earlier outcome-based educational theories for a vague or ideologically suspect emphasis on "values, attitudes and behaviors" over "knowledge, skills and other cognitive academic outcomes."[1]

Vagueness in education has posed a different policy problem to critics on the left. In higher education, where "learning outcome assessment" is now a widespread feature of curricular development and evaluation, the outcome is widely perceived as an ineffectual "administrative and regulatory necessity," write Trevor Hussey and Patrick Smith, two critics of learning outcome assessment models, rather than an insightful evaluation of "students' deep engagement with the curriculum."[2] As outcomes become mandatory bureaucratic features of syllabi and program descriptions, they become means of satisfying mandates from above: a teacher crafts learning outcomes for her course to satisfy a superior, who needs to satisfy a dean or unit chair, who has to please a president or principal, who has to prove to a superintendent or a legislature how efficiently (read: cheaply) the institution is being run. Another problem with outcomes is the timescale on which they work: the phrase "learning outcome" can often be synonymous with a day's or week's "lesson plan," as Hussey and Smith write. But in scaling up from a particular module to a semester-long class or a course of study, learning outcomes cannot help but be general, even rote recitations of general ambitions, rather than measurable tasks. In one reading, the learning outcome does not measure much of anything. Even worse, the focus on outcomes leads to a kind of educational Taylorism, write Michael Bennett and Jacqueline Brady, in which education is reduced to whatever can be measured. Where "objectives" are variable, outcomes are a "normalizing device and instrument of social regulation" geared toward imposing administrative discipline and educational standardization. In this respect, "outcomes" are the cousin of **competencies**, a definition of knowledge as a set of discrete tasks, rather than broadly applicable skills. You only need to know what you need to know at work, in other words.[3]

PASSION (N.)

Passion has long had two broad meanings in English. The first, now mostly archaic—"senses relating to physical suffering and pain," particularly of a martyr—derives from Christ's suffering at the crucifixion. The other meaning, more common today, describes a secular emotional enthusiasm, often pleasurable, which can be overpowering and sometimes, though not always, destructive.

As passion became secularized in the medieval period, it also become eroticized, and "the discourse of romance transformed passion from a pain that it was best to avoid into an experience to be sought," writes David Shumway. Nonetheless, the overpowering nature of such a powerful enthusiasm required care and discipline; a "crime of passion" is an example of the irrational excess often attached to this modern meaning. There is "no one of our natural Passions so hard to subdue as pride," writes Benjamin Franklin in his *Autobiography*, that nonetheless prideful record of a young man's rise to wealth and citizenship in the early American republic. For Franklin and many of his contemporaries, "passion" is a count noun. When it is used this way, as something to be subdued, one's passions, meaning one's drives and desires, are suspect because by being overpowering, they are also potentially controlling. For Franklin, worldly success follows from virtue, and to achieve both, our passions must be disciplined by our will. (Those familiar with Franklin's biography will know that his repeated failure to suppress his sexual passions ultimately did little harm to his worldly success.) In the romantic literature of the early twentieth century, Shumway continues, passion is pleasurable, but it lies outside of and prior to the disciplining institution of marriage—that is, romantic passion leads to marriage (and often the end of a novel) but does not necessarily define it. This helps explain a paradox in modern marriage discourse, and indeed of modern discourse around work as well: one works on a marriage and seeks passion at work.[1]

Steve Jobs is probably the figure most closely linked to the change in our assessment of passion's causal link to wealth. In a commencement address at Stanford University in 2006, the Apple executive began by recalling his own time as a student: he briefly attended Reed College before dropping out, bored by its required classes and frustrated by its high price tag. Following his "curiosity and intuition"—his desires and drives—proved more valuable than following a degree program, he told graduates. "You've got to find what you love," he advised them. "And that is as true for your work as it is for your lovers."[2] Here, the erotic and the professional passions are no longer in contradiction; they fire on the same cylinders, as it were. The workplace ideology of "do what you love" linked with Jobs has been diagnosed by Miya Tokumitsu as a "secret handshake of the privileged and a worldview that disguises its elitism as noble self-betterment." By asserting that one finds fulfillment in work, the "do what you love" ideal compels workers to identify with their jobs in ways that may undermine their interests as workers. Moreover, those who counsel workers and students to follow their passion rarely if ever acknowledge the structural obstacles to finding meaningful, enjoyable, *and* well-compensated work. Most people, it should go without saying, cannot love their jobs.[3]

But perhaps work can manage two of these, at least: it can be meaningful and enjoyable if not well-paying. Passion is often described as the force that motivates jobs affiliated with what Arlie Russell Hochschild, in her pioneering 1983 book *The Managed Heart*, called "emotional labor," jobs in which "the emotional style of offering the service is part of the service itself." Hochschild's major example was flight attendants, but emotional labor is a major part of purpose-driven jobs like nursing, teaching, and child care, professions identified largely with women and with feminized traits like caring or nurturing.[4] Such positions are often low-paid and insecure. But when we admiringly describe schoolteachers as passionate, we are, however unintentionally, describing their willingness to endure low pay and disrespect at work. Their passion and sense of mission become a kind of compensation. And while passion is something we must often perform at work, it's not a thing we necessarily feel there. Teachers and other "care workers" are said to be driven *by* a passion, but good teachers know that they too must carefully manage their enthusiasm, lest they exhaust themselves emotionally and burn out. Passion at work is still something to be managed—but often by or for someone else. "When we enter the world of profit-and-loss statements, when the psychological costs of emotional labor are not acknowledged by the company," writes Hochschild, then we may come to understand the need to perform passion as a burden that alienates us from passions we actually feel in our lives.[5]

Outside of work, passions tend to be more social, though no less disciplined. Besides romantic and sexual life, we most associate passion with fandom: small groups of people, grouped by a combination of geography, taste, and some emotional investment in a team, a hobby, or some other esoteric interest. Consider the passion of the Boston Red Sox fan, which reproduces itself through things that can be bought and sold: replica jerseys, Fenway Park souvenirs, game tickets, and so on. But it is not generated by those things: a fan's devotion is a complex of aesthetic factors *related* to but not entirely captured by those commodities, like the team's colors, the quirky architecture of the home park, geographic loyalties, and other deeply felt emotional bonds with the team, like the way a relationship with a parent or child is mediated through a shared love of the club. These are all things that distinguish a passionate fan base in Boston from one in, say, Phoenix. These elements of a passion are elusive and not easily commodifiable—if they were, Phoenix newspapers would not run regular articles bemoaning Arizona fans' lack of passion. This dilemma has not stopped marketers and management scholars from developing metrics for measuring passion, though. One scholar, a true romantic named Michael Lewis, calls passion "fan equity." Passion, therefore, is a pillar of late capitalist ideology, but passion is also a social feeling that lives on the edge of what can be captured by the **market**: passion is, as it has always been, mysterious, dangerous, and somewhat unmanageable. In other words, you can never really bottle and sell it, try though you might. And many do try: passion is the "secret sauce" for success, according to more than a few business writers, their metaphors for life's deepest mysteries apparently limited to McDonald's condiments.[6]

When passion is a requirement for individual success, as in Jobs' commencement advice, it is no longer a form of emotional compensation linked with feminized "care work." It is instead the secret sauce of better compensated executive professions. What is it about most office jobs that demands or even rewards passion, though? The secret sauce argument often refers to the zeal that must motivate **entrepreneurs** early on in a venture. But passion is also said to wane after a long run of success. The *Harvard Business Review* describes a former CEO of BFGoodrich who came to feel he "had fallen in step with a corporate culture that was focused on shareholder value in a way that was inconsistent with what he cared about." The article does not explain what the CEO cared about, nor why he should have sought it in a transnational tire corporation. What matters, instead, is that he cared about *something*—money, social justice, radial tires—not that he cared about any particular thing. In this way, passion, like **grit**, is a moral quality unmoored from any sense of ethics.[7]

Franklin might be surprised at the ways in which worldly success is now said to derive from unleashing our zealous desires, rather than suppressing them. Indeed, Jobs's embrace of his passions in issuing the bromide to "do what you love" seems to stand in contrast to Franklin's ideal of righteous management of his passions. Yet what passion's history also shows is that it is, like **innovation,** always linked to virtue. For those in the caring professions, passion is increasingly its own reward. In the business world, instead of suppressing one's passions to find worldly success, one is now asked to pursue them for the same reason. The wages of sin may still be death, but for a few of us, the wages of passion come with stock options.

PIVOT (N., V.)

The business magazine *Fast Company* runs a column called "The Pivot," which chronicles examples of bold changes in organizational direction. Zappos pivoted from facilitating shoe sales by vendors to shipping shoes itself. Barack Obama was reelected in 2012, we learn, to the imaginary office of "Pivoter-in-Chief." Detroit's municipal bankruptcy a year later was a "pivot." Pivoting, in its literal meaning, means physical agility and quickness. As an example of late-capitalist body talk, pivoting connotes the pliability needed to accommodate the **market's** demands. Besides its failure to draw any distinction between the private sector and democratic governance, *Fast Company*'s use of the pivot manifests a conflict inherent in many of these keywords, which celebrate acquiescent **flexibility** but also moral commitment and **passion.** Obama's campaign slogan emphasized change we could believe in; and Zappos's CEO didn't call his company's abrupt shift a pivot, notes Simone Baribeau in her *Fast Company* profile of company founder Tony Hsieh. She quotes Hsieh's book, *Delivering Happiness: A Path to Profits, Passion, and Purpose,* where he insists that "it was about what [we wanted] Zappos to stand for and mean in the long-term."[8]

As we have seen, the proliferation of bodily metaphors in economic writing is a feature of the naturalization of the market in capitalist culture—as if the propensity to truck, barter, and exchange resides in our bones and muscles. We can see why a corporation might want to think of itself as agile and **nimble,** springing gymnastically across the obstacles in its path, or **robust** in its confrontation with challenges. But pivoting is a peculiar metaphor for trailblazing, since literal pivoting is all about *constraints* on movement. A basketball player "pivots" by moving right or left while keeping one foot stationary. Alternatively, a pivot refers to dependence. As the *OED* says, it can be "any physical part on which another part turns"—a tool used to manipulate a larger object. This is how the word used to be employed as a political metaphor, when countries were strategic pivots in geopolitical games of strategic alliances.[9]

The word is used in US political journalism now as a verb or as a noun derived from the verb—to pivot is to shift focus or direction without substantially moving. Media coverage of President Donald Trump's first address to Congress revolved around whether or not he "pivoted" to a more "presidential" bearing, an often-asked question that was just as often mocked by critics who noted how much political pundits like to appreciate, with a discerning air of connoisseurship, superficial media exercises for which they are the major audience. This meaning of the pivot has much in common with rebranding. Corporate and personal **brands** are treated by their **makers**, paradoxically, as authentic identities, about which "stories" can be told.[10] In Trump, though, the shallowness of the concept is laid bare. He is regarded either as a thoroughly fabricated TV character, incapable of authentic conviction, or a thoroughly authentic person who "says what he thinks." So his pivots could only ever be either insincere or self-incriminating. If you're a malleable blowhard, then all you do is pivot; if you are capable of authentic conviction, then any pivot is a betrayal. When someone politically pivots, they change appearance while staying in one place. The pivot is like a beginner's magic trick: turning around in a circle, hiding the rabbit, and hoping your audience is fooled.

RESILIENCE (N.); RESILIENT (ADJ.)

A revealing fact about contemporary uses of resilience is buried in the word's etymology. Its Latin root is *resilientia,* or "fact of avoiding." From urban policy in the Global North to NGOs in the Global South, from classrooms to boardrooms, resilience is used to describe a population or an individual's strength in the face of adversity. Resilience in this modish sense is a moral quality derived from its second *OED* definition—"the quality or fact of being able to recover quickly or easily from, or resist being affected by, a misfortune, shock, illness, etc." The word's first, primary meaning is the material property of "elasticity," but resilience is increasingly a property of people rather than plastics or metals. It seems to name peoples' ability to respond and rebound from things that strike them head-on; the term's popularity, though, derives from what it lets us avoid facing more clearly.

Most scholars trace the origin of resilience as a moral or social category to the work of environmental scientist C. S. Holling. He defined it in a 1973 article as "a measure of the persistence of systems and of their ability to absorb change and disturbance and still maintain the same relationships between populations." Insofar as natural systems are also human systems, of course, Holling's concept of environmental resilience was inseparable from the human management of and reliance upon nonhuman nature. The field of "ecological economics" has applied the concept of resilience to the management of natural resources, and in the Global South, "resilience" has become a significant part of the rhetorical arsenal of "**sustainable** development."[1] It is also common in the language of humanitarian relief, where a people's resilience to crisis is thought to be proactive preparation for disaster, rather than a reactive response to it. Note the grammatical strangeness of this common phrase, "resilience to crisis," as if "resilience" is literally replacing "resistance." While there may indeed be practical benefits to planning in this way, as Julian Reid and Brad Evans write in *Resilient Life: The Art of Living Dangerously*, the problem is that we apply the word "resilient" to a population "insofar as it adapts to rather than resists the conditions of its suffering in the world." One can only be "resilient to crisis"—or, more to the point, expect others to be—if one first accepts crisis as a more or less regular condition of those others' existence. Who among the most comfortable denizens of the first world plans for crisis, or expects to be always confronting it? To be marked resilient suggests, therefore, that you reside in one of those places of regular crisis and routine suffering. Meanwhile, in the Global North, resilience is a mainstay of pseudo-scientific self-help literature that drives the **wellness** industry, in which one's physical and spiritual health is defined in terms of one's own, private ability to bounce back from hardship.[2]

To return to the Latin root: what is being evaded by the proliferation of resilience? Principally, work and exploitation. The International Monetary Fund argues that the most resilient economies have the most **flexible** labor and commodity markets; resilient here seems, like flexible, to be a euphemism for vulnerable, precarious, non-unionized. In addition, like wellness or flexibility, resilience is a receding horizon, and the work of building it can never end. That is, one can always be more well, flexible, or resilient. Resilience has been taken up enthusiastically in executive publications like *Fast Company* and *Harvard Business Review*, which produce endless lists of the five, ten, or seven habits of resilient executives, employees, or companies. "Why do some people and some companies buckle under pressure?" asks an author in one *Harvard Business Review* guide to resilience. "And what makes others bend and ultimately bounce back?" The rather tautological conclusion, of course, is that some entrepreneurs are resilient and can bend and bounce back—that's how you know they are resilient, after all.[3] As with **innovation** and **excellence,** the tautologies of business propaganda function like a wagon circle keeping out criticism.

In humanitarian and development discourse, on the other hand, resilience is invoked to praise an impoverished population for its strength in the face of hardship. Such professions of sympathy, however sincere or well intentioned, can become powerfully cynical if they do not consider history, power, and the distance between the resilient subject and the person or institution calling them such. This is the point of a much-circulated poster in post-Katrina New Orleans, which bore a quotation attributed to a local lawyer, Tracie Washington: "Every time you say, 'Oh, they're so resilient,' that means you can do something else to me." In New Orleans, Washington's quote suggests, resilience became a way of assessing the post-disaster situation sentimentally without responding to it politically. In praising the resilient population's ability to bear pressure, Sarah Ahmed has written elsewhere, resilience allows space for yet more pressure. To cite another recent example: the USAID called Haitians "the most resilient people on earth" after the country's devastating 2010 earthquake, which seems like an allusion not just to the disaster response but to the country's famous history of revolt. Swap "resilient" for "oppressed" or "revolutionary," though, and you would have quite a different USAID press release.[4]

The heroic narrative of Black suffering that has emerged out of New Orleans and Haiti, the capacity to resiliently "endure," as William Faulkner put it in *The Sound and the Fury*, has a very long history in the United States. In "Many Thousands Gone," James Baldwin regarded the Faulknerian admiration for the resilience of African American Southerners as a kind of sentimental abuse intended to comfort white onlookers. Baldwin described Aunt Jemima and Uncle Tom, those depthless objects of white affection, as "prodigies of resilience" preternaturally gifted with the power to endure pain. Many common uses of resilience like-wise seem to tell us as much about the speaker of the praise as they do about its object. After all, we would be hard-pressed to name the people who responded to a devastating hurricane or earthquake with unresilient cowardice and weakness.[5]

Its slippery usage, suggested by its Latin root, also derives from its mixed material and moral meanings. The earliest uses of resilience were in engineering, where it referred to the flexibility or elasticity of an object. Only later was it applied figuratively by Holling to an ecosystem's capacity to absorb change. The current voguish use of population resilience is therefore a metaphor for a metaphor: resilient people borrow the capacities of **ecosystems** to recover from crisis, and this ecological meaning was in turn borrowed from an object's ability to bend. What was lost along the way was Holling's rather limited application: a resilient biological system does not "bounce back," as a ball springing off a resilient object would; nor does it recover its original state, as a resilient piece of putty might. Rather, it simply persists in an altered but basically intact state. It doesn't break, but this doesn't mean it is not damaged.

The bestselling book *Resilience: Why Things Bounce Back,* which received the imprimatur of the *New York Times* op-ed page, shows how elastic the term can be. Although their subtitle defines resilience as "bouncing back," authors Andrew Zolli and Ann Marie Healy define the term in their book more narrowly, as "the capacity of a system, enterprise, or a person to maintain its core purpose and integrity in the face of dramatically changed circumstances," which conflates three very different things—complex systems, specific firms, and individuals. Zolli and Healey begin with an anecdote from the Mexico City tortilla riots of 2007. As they argue, the uprising erupted after world corn prices skyrocketed, drastically increasing the local price of tortillas. Although they recognize the role of US corn subsidies, NAFTA, and ethanol production in inflating local corn prices, the authors attribute the riots to the effect of Hurricane Katrina, which damaged oil refineries and encouraged the planting of more ethanol corn. NAFTA and American agribusiness are treated not as political circumstances but as metaphorical storms: since "we cannot control the volatile tides of change," they write, "we can learn to build better boats."[6] These examples are all part of a long tradition of naturalizing our contemporary political and economic order, treating food shortages and layoffs as if they are acts of nature that can never change. Resilience, once a property of the environment, has become a property of people. And those most vulnerable to the environmental shocks associated with modern capitalism are also responsible for becoming more resilient against them.

ROBUST (ADJ.)

"Tender and delicate persons have so many things to trouble them," wrote Francis Bacon in 1625, "which more robust natures have little sense of." Two centuries later, when the New York City preacher and author Thomas de Witt Talmage visited Boston, he was impressed by its people's constitutions. "When a mutton chop is swallowed of a Bostonian it gives up," he wrote in *Around the Tea-Table*, "knowing that there is no need of fighting against such inexorable digestion." For the women of Boston, it is no longer fashionable to be "delicate." Instead, wrote Talmage, "they are robust in mind and always ready for an argument."[7]

Robust is not often used this way anymore to describe people's minds and bodies: now, it is most common as an economic term, almost always accompanied by "growth" or "economy," or as a way of marketing olive oil, wine, or coffee. It connotes strength without sounding uncouth. For example: when south Philadelphia's Edward Bok Vocational School, a WPA-built public school, was closed after deep cuts in state funding to Philadelphia's public schools, it was turned into a craft-beer bar and "incubator" for what its new owners called "Do-It-Yourself (**DIY**) innovators, artists and **entrepreneurs**." Bok is a "robust" structure, built to last, read promotional materials for the new building.

Instead of teachers and students, though, its sturdy joists and hardwood floors now support "a critical mass of **creatives**." To take another example: Penn State's English department, anxious that students and parents see a literature degree as professionally weak, described its curriculum as "robust." It is also a popular political term of art and to describe the "robust debate" that politicians always say they welcome.[8]

In the nineteenth century (and the first half of the twentieth) "robust's" collocates—the words appearing most often alongside it—were "constitution," "vigorous," "ruddy," "healthy," and "manly." It was a moral attribute, legible in the male body. "Only robust teachers for Chicago," declared a 1900 *New York Times* story pinpointing teachers' "physical weakness" as the city schools' biggest flaw. "Robust growth," meanwhile, was a phrase more likely to be found in a seed catalog advertising vigorous flower bulbs than a newspaper reporting the business news. When applied to people, robust's association with manliness made it a popular adjective to describe military life. Imperial British soldiers were "stout and robust," and military service would make a man out of nearly anyone, even on the losing side. One Confederate veteran reflected in his Civil War memoir that Confederate States army soldiering was at least fortifying: "many a weak, puny boy was returned to his parents a robust, healthy, manly man," he wrote.[9]

Robustness began to be associated with national economies only after World War II; this usage surged in the 1980s and reached its current popularity in the late 1990s. Ronald Reagan's economic advisors were fond of the term, invoking it with regularity as the 1982 and 1983 budgets were released amidst a recession. Robust's usage for the US economy tracks with such moments of crisis. Writing of Ronald Reagan's 1982 budget, *US News and World Report* wrote that "the President's advisers predict that a brisk snapback from the recession, beginning in the spring, will launch the economy on several years of robust, uninterrupted growth." More recently, the BBC asked, "Is the US economy sufficiently robust to begin the return to normality?"

"What the US can't live without is robust economic growth," said the Democratic political strategist David Axelrod in 2010. Its old militarist roots help explain its popularity with nativists like the popular British neofascist blogger David Vance, who recently urged the European Union to follow "the robust approach of Hungary" in expelling and jailing refugees. And in a throwback to the nineteenth century, one Fox News host called for a "more robust, manly version of Christianity" to defeat ISIS.[10]

The virile connotations endure even for those off the racist right. A robust economy is like a fit, stout paterfamilias who provides for all the nation's children. Robust growth is equally shared, in the way that an expanding balloon or Dad's vigorous potbelly is fattest around the middle. Robust, like **nimble**, **lean**, and **flexible**, is a keyword that imagines the firm, or the abstraction we call "the economy," as a body. Robust describes the growth objective; lean, nimble, and flexible describe the kinds of workers that are required to achieve it. A robust economy is a hungry beast, with inexorable digestion. It takes nimble workers to feed it.

SHARE (V.); SHARING (ADJ.)

When we learn how to do it in kindergarten, sharing has a straightforwardly positive meaning. When it is used as a modifier of the word "economy," however, its meaning becomes muddied and controversial, even for the most enthusiastic intellectual defenders of what is also called "crowd-based," "peer-to-peer," or "platform" capitalism. In his 2016 book *The Sharing Economy,* the economist Arun Sundararajan disavows his own title. "We may be losing a good verb," he admits, conceding that nobody's conventional definition of sharing—"to perform, enjoy, or suffer in common with others"—fits the business model of Uber, Lyft, or Airbnb. (Except perhaps the suffering part.)[1]

Sundararajan says he persists with "sharing economy" because of the phrase's currency. But even that may be fading. A regular feature of mainstream news articles on these sorts of businesses is a prefatory comment about what exactly to call them. Calling businesses like Uber or Airbnb "peer-to-peer," "platform," or "crowd" services emphasizes their technological novelty; the "gig economy," meanwhile, underscores the work done on those "platforms," with the old-fashionedness of the word "gig" serving as an implicit rejoinder to the techno-utopianism of platform enthusiasts. Where "gig" names labor, sharing emphasizes ownership, of one's house, car, or information (as in the sharing one does on social media sites) or one's body (in the case of the labor-sharing service TaskRabbit). The fact that the asset may not actually be owned by the sharer, as in a rented apartment subleased on Airbnb, only emphasizes the most important feature of sharing as an adjective: this is the word's abstraction from the actual economic relations of the industries it purports to describe. Sharing suggests a flattening of old hierarchies. Rather than the vertically integrated companies of yore, which controlled their material assets and supply chains and directly employed many thousands of workers, the "sharing economy" purports to offer horizontal access to a disaggregated "platform" that serves as a medium for sharing. Uber, for example, is not a taxi company (so it says); it simply runs an app that puts riders in touch with drivers. Rather than "the twentieth-century model where the corporation accumulates resources and produces goods and services," goes a glowing report from the Brookings Institution India, the sharing economy offers a "twenty-first-century model where we can avail certain platforms." Besides modernity, therefore, sharing implies agency and self-determination for the worker. No wonder, then, that sharing economy corporations like Uber like to call their low-wage independent contractors "transportation **entrepreneurs**," in defiance of the dictionary and of common sense.[2]

Sharing also connotes "trust," which for sharing economy apologists is one of its greatest social advantages. In opening their personal spaces and private vehicles to strangers, this argument goes, Airbnb hosts and Lyft drivers are sharing not only their private property, but some aspect of themselves. As Sundararajan insists, in a moment of the fevered utopianism that can sometimes afflict members of the economics profession, the for-profit sharing economy might "organically weave greater levels of connectedness into our everyday economic activities . . . and create new social contexts to replace the ones Durkheim lamented we lost through the Industrial Revolution." On Uber, such connectedness is mediated through the ratings systems with which users assess their driver. "Trust" replaces the disciplinary function of government agencies supervising labor law and taxi medallions with a kind of egalitarian solidarity. But as Tom Slee has argued in a critical book on the sharing economy, Uber's reputation system mostly earns four and five stars for its drivers, since users typically give their drivers good ratings—most passengers, it seems, don't want to be snitches. Passengers' misuse of the ratings system is ironically one of the only truly **collaborative** aspects of the for-profit sharing economy.[3]

The danger that faces any writer on the sharing economy is technological determinism—accepting the companies' own exuberant claims on futurity and presuming too easily that smartphone technologies are the drivers, rather than a subsidiary feature, of the social and economic effects of the gig economy. Here, it is helpful to think against the tendency to see sharing-economy platforms as new, a perhaps counterintuitive approach, given the seeming novelty of the apps we use to access them. As curious and even pleasant as it may be to climb into a private car hailed though a smartphone app, all we have done is used a proprietary tool to hail a taxi. And if labor is made more precarious via the Uber-like model of extracting rents from subcontractors bound by this tool, this is less of a technological novelty than a return to older economic models—whether you're using a smartphone or an oxcart, it's still tenant labor.

If the technology behind the sharing economy is not the source of its dominance, though, what is? "Financialization" may be the most relevant answer. "Finance, at its most basic level," writes the cultural critic Alison Shonkwiler, "is the domain in which value is less likely to be *produced* than captured and/or extracted, typically by managing a degree of risk." The "financialization" of the economy is the orientation of capital accumulation (i.e., making money from the labor of others) around this extraction of value. Shonkwiler, following critics like David Harvey, argues that financialization is what is really new about the economy of the turn of the twenty-first century.[4] In the sharing economy, neither cars nor homes nor technologies are produced; instead, rents are extracted from assets owned by others. According to Michael Spence, an NYU economist, the sharing economy's motive is "exploiting under-utilized resources—be they physical and financial capital or **human capital** and talent."[5] The beating heart of the sharing economy is not the collaborative spirit of its workers—rather, that spirit is one of the undervalued assets to be stripped.

SMART (ADJ.)

Smart, used as an adjective modifying a technology, connotes an efficient, clean, orderly pragmatism. Smartness is above human prejudices and unruly **passions**. Smartness just *works*. Smart technologies, from munitions to ID cards to refrigerators to mattresses, usually do one of three related things, and often all three: they allow (or require) a user to remotely access a computer-linked network, they generate **data** about that user, and they act autonomously, or seem to do so. By accessing a computer network with a smart card, we can access our health insurance data; by using a smart thermostat or smart bed, we can turn up the heat from anywhere with an internet connection and monitor our breathing and restlessness overnight. Smart-as-autonomous got its start in the Vietnam War, as a way of describing laser-guided bombs that the US military dropped on Hanoi, long before the newer, video-enabled generation of the early 1990s became a main attraction of prime-time Persian Gulf war coverage. The Air Force called the smart bombs it dropped on North Vietnam "hobos," an ironic portmanteau of "homing bombs" that has not survived. Instead of relying on human targeting, these smart bombs were "guided by a television picture or a laser beam on to its target," according to a contemporary news report, and were heralded as a "technological revolution" that would dramatically change warfare. By maximizing efficiency in the destruction of targets, the argument went, the smart bomb would enable the US Navy and Air Force to cut their bomber fleets—an early example of smart technologies as workplace automation, long before E-Z Pass put a single tollbooth worker out of a job.[6]

Smart buildings were the next major development in smart technologies, first appearing in news coverage in 1985, when the National Association of Homebuilders began an experimental Smart House venture. Smart House engineers promised that "within a few years, a telephone call might be made to the Smart House before leaving the work place in order to have the house cooled and dinner cooking by the time a working couple got home." This is, essentially, the promise of today's smart house devices, like Nest (the smartphone-enabled thermostat) and Echo (the Amazon "smart home hub" that lets you remotely operate your home's lights or smoke alarms.) The major difference is the kind of phone (a smart one, naturally) that we now use to control the technology. Smart therefore now most often describes a device that is connected to an online network and, in its ability to generate and retain data, seems to have a memory. The military origins of smart technologies and their pre-internet transition to civilian life show that the smartness of a device lies in the possibility of efficient, remote manipulation. While some modern smart devices are said to learn the preferences of their human masters, the suggestion here is not that the devices themselves have a brain, but that they are connected to yours. In addition, smart means modern. The six thousand dollar smart refrigerator that tells you when you're out of milk shows that the key to a smart technology isn't whether it is, in fact, a wise idea. To be smart is simply to belong to the new age.[7]

The word's sense of unbiased reasonableness and basic goodness means that any type of smart technology, like an **innovative** one, is thought by definition to be worthwhile. Smart therefore presumes the political neutrality of the technologies we use. The technology critic Evgeny Morozov describes how a seemingly benign example of smart technology, the parking systems designed to maximize parking revenue by connecting parking fares to particular vehicles, ends up inhibiting the agency of citizens by making the work of government—even work as unloved as that done by the parking authority—more opaque and manipulative. "A truly smart system," Morozov writes, "would find a way to turn us into more reflective, caring, and humane creatures."[8] Besides offering a benign veneer for advanced forms of value extraction, smart technologies also facilitate what its users and designers were already doing—by making something faster, cheaper, more deadly, or more profitable—instead of transforming our sense of what is possible, or wise.

SOLUTION (N.)

The usage of "solutions" in the plural to describe a business venture became popular in the 1990s, as a consequence of a burgeoning software industry. But it was already in use in the telecommunications industry. In 1979, the company Network Solutions was founded, and later went on to earn the first government contract to assign web addresses. A search of classified ads in the *New York Times* shows the plural noun's regular use in the business world in the mid-80s; GE Information Services, which advertised itself as the "total solution" to your sales expectations, also solicited employees for "**innovative** systems solutions."[9]

The word has much of the same allure and benevolence as **smart**. Solutions are here to fix whatever needs fixing; a solution, by definition, requires a problem. The keyword solutions responds to two common problems raised by technology, especially computing and software: that it is inscrutable, and that it is dangerous. Solutions addresses the first by mystifying a company's actual service or function: if you had attempted to describe in its name what Network Solutions actually did when it earned the contract to assign web domains, it would have sounded more confusing and less impressive than "solutions" did. (On the other hand, framing familiar tasks as "solutions" can be a way of approximating an inscrutability that is unnerving, but also prestigious. So if you are Xerox, "business solutions" certainly is sexier than "copy machine supplies.") Second, the rise of solutions, as with **best practices** and **competencies**, exemplifies the increasing separation in corporate culture (and everything shaped in its image) of practices and technologies from their products and effects. This presumption of technological value-neutrality is only enhanced by the soporific blandness of "solutions." Morozov has called this private-sector technophilia "solutionism": an ideology that recasts "all complex social situations either as neatly defined problems with definite, computable solutions or as transparent and self-evident processes that can be easily optimized." It is a perspective that sees a world full of problems it imagines as straight nails in need of a profitable new hammer. It invents new problems and sometimes exacerbates old ones, whether through the automation that technology facilitates, which exacerbates the problem of unemployment, or the surveillance that its **data**-generation procedures perform, which creates new crises of privacy rights and freedom of speech.[10]

STAKEHOLDER (N.)

Stakeholder's primary meaning in the *OED* is "an independent person or organization with whom money is deposited, esp. when a number of people make a bet or other financial transaction." It is thus financial, even speculative—notice the particular link to gambling, which was one of the most common nineteenth-century uses of the word. A stakeholder is the person or group with whom others' money is deposited, often a third party or trustee. More recently, it has become commonly used by nonprofit voluntary organizations, in education, community development, and other sectors. Here, a stakeholder is anyone with an interest (a metaphorical "stake") in the success of an organization or venture.

The concept of the stakeholder in management theory is often credited to the Harvard Law School professor E. Merrick Dodd, who did not pioneer the use of the word itself (that honor belongs to two later management theorists, R. Edward Freeman and Ian Mitroff, in the early 1980s) but outlined its meaning in a 1932 *Harvard Law Review* article. In the midst of the Depression, Dodd argued for more responsible corporate practices, recognizing that public opinion was turning against the view that a corporation's only obligation was to its shareholders. Dodd argued that corporate managers have obligations not only to shareholders, but to their firm's employees, customers, and the general public. In the political climate of the Depression, when calls for economic planning and socialism reached a high point, a conflict between the interests of the stockholders and everyone else was brewing. The notion of the stakeholder derives from this Depression-era notion of the "socially responsible" corporation. We can see the stakeholder concept here as a response to class conflict: instead of the clash of labor and capital, what about a meeting of stakeholders?[11]

As a term of organizational ethics, stakeholder theory makes a pretty simple claim. Managers of a firm have an obligation to all those with a "stake" in it, whether that stake be fiduciary or circumstantial. The concept is vague, as many critics have pointed out, given the difficulty of defining (and ranking) a stakeholder in a particular organization.[12] One can read the invocation to take others' stakes into consideration as ill-defined at best, given the competing interests of management and employees. More ungenerous critics might read it as little more than a plea that business leaders not act like sociopaths. In British political rhetoric, the notion of the "stakeholder economy" was popularized by Tony Blair's New Labour government as an ideal of upward mobility that foregrounds individual initiative and opportunity. The stakeholder economy is "not about giving power to corporations or unions or interest groups," Blair said. Rather, "It is about giving power to you the individual." In Blair's usage, the stakeholder idea approaches most clarity about the bad things that it is not: Blair declared the British Tories to be partisans of the "no-stake economy." In American political discourse, on the other hand, "stakeholders" are embraced by politicians like New York governor Andrew Cuomo, to suggest the participants in an unrancourous, collegial, bipartisan style of governance. Americans also use it as a term of critique for rival powers like China, which is urged to shape up and be a more "responsible stakeholder in the global system"—like the United States presumably is. While other synonyms exist for those who facilitate bets and investments, stakeholder seems increasingly

essential as an organizational word. Individual organizations have particular terms for their membership or staff, of course. Labor unions have members, but there is no other term to refer in common to the workers in a factory, the employees of the restaurant down the street from the factory, the teachers at the workers' children's school, and so on. Referring to all these players as common "stakeholders," of course, implies that they share interests and a common stake. And in many respects, they may. But here we would do well to remember the financial origins of the term: some stakes are bigger than others.[13]

As a term of political and business rhetoric that conceals its financial origins in a vocabulary of participatory cooperation, stakeholder belongs to an age of heightening inequality, true to its 1930s origins. Like other phrases derived from gambling and finance that have migrated into democratic politics—the appropriately gruesome phrase "skin in the game" comes to mind—stakeholder conflates access with rights, obscuring hierarchies of power under the veneer of **collaboration**.

SUSTAINABLE (ADJ.) SUSTAINABILITY (N.)

"Sustainable" is an old word in English, which once referred negatively to an emotional burden one could endure; it has also been a synonym of "provable," in a legal sense (as in the legal-drama courtroom exclamation, "objection sustained!"). These either obsolete or technical usages have given way to the more general, common meaning, "capable of being maintained or continued at a certain rate or level." For this contemporary definition the *OED* gives mostly economic examples, and indeed "sustainable" was until quite recently used to refer to "steady" economic growth, with none of the ethical or environmental meanings we now associate with the term. "The Big Three's first-quarter production plans look more sustainable now than they did a month ago," wrote the *Wall Street Journal* in 1986, referring only to car sales projections, not gas mileage or carbon footprints.[14]

Since the turn of the last century, the adjective has been used to mean "capable of being maintained," often with an implied reference to the natural environment. As a marketing term, it is suggestive of technological **innovation** along with a sense of moral conscientiousness and forward thinking.[15] The contemporary conservationist meaning of sustainable tracks with the rise of the noun form "sustainability," a word almost unknown before the 1980s. The *Corpus of Historical American English* shows no uses of the term before this decade.[16] Google's ngram database offers just a handful of examples, mostly Defense Department memos and other bureaucratic documents lacking public circulation. The coinage of sustainability correlates with the rise of "sustainable development," a conservationist critique of development economics that emphasizes the frailty of nature, or what the World Bank in its charming way calls "natural capital."[17]

The United Nations has helped define and popularize sustainable development in various summits and proclamations: the 1987 Brundtland Report defined it as "development that meets the needs of the present without compromising the ability of future generations to meet their own needs."[18] The word came into broad circulation after the 1992 Rio Earth Summit, which made sustainability a byword of environmental policymaking. The first principle listed in the Rio Summit's report, called "Agenda 21," proposed that "human beings are at the center of concerns for sustainable development. They are entitled to a healthy and productive life in harmony with nature."[19] "Sustainable" has the advantage of being unambiguously good—who wants to be exhaustible?—and invitingly vague. It can accommodate Marxist economists and neo-Malthusian doomsday cranks, mining companies and environmentalists. BP is committed to sustainability, and has a website to prove it. In a happy coincidence, sustaining Earth's ecology and sustaining BP's shareholder dividends are two sides of the same sustainable coin: "the best way for BP to achieve sustainable success as a company," BP's website reads, "is to act in the long-term interests of our shareholders, our partners and society."[20] This combination of ethical straightforwardness *in theory*—we must be responsible stewards of natural resources for future generations—and subjective imprecision *in practice* is the source of much of its popularity, as critics have pointed out.[21] The word is an inherently subjective term, meaningful only in comparison to something that is less sustainable than the object in question. And then there is the temporal lag of counterevidence: the final proof that our current practices are actually unsustainable will not come until after we are dead.

So, sustainability, like innovation and **stakeholder**, compensates for literal vagueness with moral certainty. And like **resilience**, it is a relative term, which allows it to be used opportunistically. The question for those who use it then becomes: sustainable for whom, and for how long? As a lifestyle and marketing term, sustainable can paradoxically express the same capitalist triumphalism—of an ever-expanding horizon of goods and services, of growth without consequences—that the conservationist concept was once meant to critique. "Sustainable development," fuzzy as it was, was intended to remind us of the limited supply and unequal exploitation of Earth's natural resources. But if sustainability is only ever comparative, and if it most literally means an ability to keep on doing something, its popularity as a consumerist value suggests that there is a fine line between "sustainable" and "complacent."

SYNERGY (N.)

In the *OED,* "synergy" is defined in two major ways. Firstly, as "join action" or "cooperation," with a particular theological connotation: "cooperation between human will and divine grace in the work of regeneration." The second meaning is the more familiar one: "any interaction or cooperation which is mutually reinforcing; a dynamic, productive, or profitable affinity, association, or link." Its use in business circles peaked in the 1990s and early 2000s, when "synergy" meant organizational harmony and the achievement of a unity that is greater than the sum of its parts. Mergers, for example, were thought to bring synergy (or occasionally "synergies") to companies that lacked economies of scale or critical product lines on their own. It is the only word on this list that could be called obsolete in the business world; the word is regarded as something of a relic and is regularly featured in business-press articles on buzzwords to avoid. Synergy's career is an example of the disposability of the business wisdom that is nonetheless peddled as time-tested truth. One consultant interviewed by *Forbes* complained that synergy "never fails to make me think of my wife's childhood obsession with Jem and the Holograms," the stars of *Jem,* the 1980s cartoon that featured a shape-shifting hologram machine named Synergy. More on this later.[22]

Early meanings of synergy were usually biological, referring to the coordinated action driving organic bodies and cells, like the synergy of human gestation. Synergy's other meaning was theological, referring in a Protestant sense to the "cooperation between human will and divine grace." If **innovation** once referred negatively to the sinful hubris of self-appointed prophets, synergy was its virtuous opposite: the humble copartnership of human and divine effort. The word came into wider use in the twentieth century via Lester Ward, an ex-botanist and paleontologist who became the first president of the American Sociological Association. A self-taught disciple of the positivist thinker Auguste Comte, Ward used synergy to describe a governing principle of all social structures. Synergy, he argued, was the dynamic clash of opposing forces in nature, as well as in human societies.[23] Ward saw synergy as a biological principle that also shaped the laws of social organization and human history. His descendants in the popular press include writers like Steven Johnson, whose bestsellers in the popular-science-cum-business-advice genre include *Where Good Ideas Come From: The Natural History of Innovation*, in which he argues that there are seven typologies for optimal, innovation-friendly environments, which can be observed across nature and across time. Bill O'Connor of the Innovation Genome Project, an organization whose name also suggests a biological drive to innovate, argues that in all of human history, there have only been seven kinds of questions that have driven all innovations. The popularity of the sacramental number seven, however, suggests that cultural, rather than scientific, influences may be predominant here.[24]

Synergy's second vogue arrived in the 1960s, as a term for the grand possibilities of modern technology. A 1966 *New Yorker* profile of Buckminster Fuller introduces readers to the eccentric inventor's modernist conviction that technological advances could render obsolete the social problems of penury and waste. Synergy, or what Fuller called "synergetics," was the science and faith of this conviction. The example Fuller gave was chromium-nickel-iron alloys, which together—in synergistic combination—held up against much more intense heat than their constitutive elements could have done.[25] There was a degree of serendipity in these unpredictable, invisible chemical patterns, and the social possibilities they might allow were consequential. Alloy steel's resistance to heat made it very popular for the twentieth-century war machine, Fuller lamented. But if this synergy were applied not to weaponry, but to housing and education—what Fuller called "livingry"—it could work wonders. Post-war synergy gained further currency in the work of the psychologist Abraham Maslow, who also has a prominent place in the history of **creativity**. Maslow used synergy to describe the harmonization of the interests of an employee and his boss at work. Borrowing his use of the term from the anthropologist Ruth Benedict, Maslow defined synergy as

> the social-institutional arrangements which fuse selfishness and unselfishness, by transcending their oppositeness and polarity so that the dichotomy between selfishness and altruism is resolved and transcended and formed into a new higher unity.[26]

To return to *Jem* and its teenage protagonist, Jerrica: thanks to her father's invention, the machine named Synergy, Jerrica could, with a tug of her earring, transform herself and her two friends into a holographic projection of a glamorous rock group called Jem and the Holograms. Like Jerrica's alter ego, Maslow's version of workplace synergy is often just a mask. While much business jargon, like jargon of any kind, appears meaningless to outsiders, the real meaning it produces is not always in the words themselves, but in the disguise it creates—that is, the group identity the words create among those who know and use them. But, also like a mask, jargon often hides its meaning. So, what is business synergy hiding?

Maslow's "higher unity" ideal was already rolling eyes in 1989, when a journalist in the *New York Times* quoted a McKinsey executive who cut to the chase by admitting that "synergy in most cases is another name for head-count reductions." ("Head-count reductions," of course, is another name for "you're fired.") This is where synergy enters the vocabulary of late capitalism. Unlike **lean**, **flexible**, and **nimble** management, which are ways of dressing up the vulnerability and disposability of workers in a language of efficiency, synergy dresses up the vulnerability of executives in a language of unity. For this reason, its exuberant usage was always defensive, tinged with a bit of dread. One anonymous investor in 1989 put it this way in the *New York Times* piece that introduced "synergy" to the mainstream reader: "'All this management gobbledygook is to mask the real issue,'" he said, "'which is that these companies are afraid of being taken over by someone who will get rid of the current crop of executives.'"[27]

As Jem says when she meets Synergy for the first time: "It's not real . . . it's an illusion!"

THOUGHT LEADER (N.)

The thought leader exemplifies the ideal of individualistic, acquisitive, self-commodifying capitalist selfhood also modeled by the **entrepreneur** and the **innovator**. The major difference among the three is that while anyone, theoretically, can innovate, not just any Tom, Dick, Harry, or Sheryl can be a thought leader. The thought leader is singular and exceptional. In this sense, popular conceptions of **leadership** as a widespread trait, which schools and organizations should be in the business of cultivating in students and employees, do not apply to *thought leadership*, an obviously related but significantly different concept. Thought leadership has more in common with the older phrase, "men of industry." That is, thought leadership broadcasts the elitist impulses that leadership, entrepreneurship, and innovation often conceal behind a democratic front of accessibility. David Sessions reads the thought leader as the organic intellectual of the one percent: that is, a figure who gives this class a sense of its purpose in society. This thought leader's mission, Sessions argues convincingly, is "to mirror, systematize, and popularize the delusions of the superrich: that they have earned their fortunes on merit, that social protections need to be further eviscerated to make everyone more **flexible** for 'the future,' and that local attachments and alternative ways of living should be replaced by an aspirational consumerism."[1] And while thought leadership has the hackneyed air of an overused recent coinage, it is, like innovation, an old concept that thinks it is utterly new.

Many histories of the term credit it mistakenly to Joel Kurtzman, a prolific business-press editor and writer who began using
it in 1995 to preface interviews with corporate movers and shak-
ers in his *Strategy + Business* magazine. Kurtzman, to give him
credit, certainly popularized the concept in its current form.
Business success is a "mental game," he wrote, and "C.E.O.'s
and their top leadership teams must not only outexecute their
rivals, they must also outthink them." Thought leaders are gifted
with a kind of second sight here; where others react to events,
they anticipate the future and plan accordingly. But Kurtzman,
whether he knew it or not, was using an old phrase that dates
to the late nineteenth century. Then, the title of thought leader
connoted moral authority above all. In 1899, the Rev. J. O. M.
Hewitt described him as a model of sophistication and discipline:
"the thought leader of the race must be a man of self-control,
of mature and reasonable speech." The phrase's first example in
the *OED* comes from Lyman Abbott's flattering biography of
Henry Ward Beecher, the famous Brooklyn clergyman who became embroiled in a notorious 1875 adultery trial. Abbott, a
Beecher ally and fellow pastor, wrote his biography to exonerate
his friend. Despite the well-publicized scandal, Abbott argued,
Beecher "retains his position as the most eminent preacher and
one of the great thought leaders in America," while his "accuser"
languished in obscurity. Henry Nehemiah Dodge, an author of
Christian and historical verse around the turn of the twentieth
century, penned an ode to Christ, the first thought leader, in his
1899 *Christus Victor*:

> Thy peerless word, sweet-voiced in every tongue,
>   Invites the sons of every clime;
> Thought-Leader Thou, earth's great among,
>   Ideal of all time.

A thought leader was a moral exemplar, whose sweet-voiced elo-
quence inspired devotion and whose model behavior encouraged
imitation.[2]

Thought leadership achieved its secular meaning in the middle of the twentieth century, when it was most often a public

relations term or a way to describe experts in business and political affairs. In August 1963, a *New York Times* ad for *Atlas,* a subscription service collating translated news reports from around the world, appealed to aspiring elites: "If you're ready to join the foreign affairs experts, the thought leaders, the people who want their ideas first-hand, start your introductory subscription now," the ad copy read. *The Statist,* a British newsmagazine, advertised authoritative reviews of world affairs and global finance authored by Europe's "thought leaders."

The phrase has obviously lost the explicitly religious and moral signification it had in the nineteenth century, but like innovation, it has not shed the prophetic air that originally came with it. "A thought leader," writes a business author in a typical definition, "is someone who looks at the future and sets a course for it that others will follow."[3] And so while the term now describes a particular kind of ruling-class business intelligentsia, thought leadership is less a radical break in the tradition of the American public intellectual than the heir to some of its oldest exemplars: the adulterous moralist, the Cold War foreign policy expert, and the American thinker who thinks he charts the course, as the poet wrote, for "the sons of every clime."

WELLNESS (N.)

"Wellness" dates to the seventeenth century in English, but it is a staple of the vocabulary of the health-care industry as well as American "human-resources" departments. The word's transformation is captured in the two meanings the *OED* gives. "Wellness" has evolved from a contrastive quality—that is, as the opposite of illness—to a positive quality, a state of "good physical, mental, and spiritual health, esp. as an actively pursued goal."

The problem raised by this distinction, of course, is "good physical, mental, and spiritual health" is much harder to quantify or even to ascertain without its opposite. An 1887 Unitarian newspaper used "wellness" in its original sense, "the absence of sickness," in a sarcastic way that actually anticipates the contemporary meaning, as a quality you can never have enough of. The editorial asked the reader to pray for the "spiritual paralytics" that are prostrated on "sofas of wellness." The joke here, is that comfort can be its own anxious, incurable affliction. But for most, wellness had a relatively simple meaning: to be well meant to be not sick. Six decades later, Halbert Dunn, a physician at the US Office for Vital Statistics, coined the new term. In his 1959 article "High-Level Wellness for Man and Society," Dunn argued that the medical profession's emphasis on the prevention of illness had ignored "a fascinating and ever-changing panorama of life itself, inviting exploration of its every dimension." "Wellness" is Dunn's term for this panorama, a combination of spiritual, psychological, and physiological health. With "wellness," Dunn aimed to restore to the self a sense of integrity he saw lacking in modern society. Wellness is nourished by what Dunn calls "the **creative** spirit," an "expression of self" he understands in individual, and inward-looking, terms. "With creative expression," he writes, "comes intense inner satisfaction." Then, in a move that appears to anticipate the Orientalist trappings of later, New Age-inspired wellness doctrines, Dunn describes wellness as a harmonious blending of body and spirit. He attributes the medical profession's inability to move beyond the sickness/unsickness duality to a failing of "Western culture," its cleavage of the physiological and the spiritual:

> As if we could divide the sum total of man thus! . . . In fact, the essence of the task ahead might well be to fashion a rational bridge between the biological nature of man and the spirit of man—the spirit being that intangible something that transcends physiology and psychology.

The task is especially urgent, Dunn explains, because in a world whose population is getting older, larger, more anxious, and more desperate for ever-dwindling resources, "it is probably a fallacy for us to assume, as so many of us have done, that an expansion in scientific knowledge can indefinitely counterbalance the rapidly dwindling natural resources of the globe." Measuring wellness will be a challenge, Dunn concedes, given the abstract nature of the concept. "Since the nature of this goal is ever changing and ever expanding, we will probably never reach it in absolute terms," he writes, somewhat apologetically—but it is this boundless aspect of wellness that has led to its enduring popularity.[1]

Wellness thus emerges out of a sense of pessimism about modernity, but what has endured is its open-ended positivity. Today's sunnier culture of wellness promotion was popularized by Dr. John Travis, a physician who founded the Wellness Resource Center in 1975 in Marin County, CA. "Wellness isn't a term you hear everyday," said Dan Rather in a 1979 *60 Minutes* report on Travis and his Center. Wellness is "self-care" and an "an ongoing state of growth" both physical and spiritual, Travis explained to

Rather. "Our goal," he said, "is to help the person discover *why* they are sick." As an "ongoing state of growth," wellness names a task that can never be completed. While it's possible to say, or at least to feel, that you are no longer ill, you can always be more "well" than you are. This might actually enhance the stress wellness is supposed to address, as one becomes ever more anxious about one's failure to become less anxious.[2]

In Rather's *60 Minutes* report, he asked a group at the Wellness Resource Center to respond to criticism that wellness was "a middle-class cult." One woman responded that if wellness was a cult, it was one in which "you're the **leader**, you're your own guru." The rhetoric of personal autonomy in wellness culture, and its faintly rebellious critique of the health-care establishment, recalls the origins of **maker** culture in Northern California around the same time, and one can argue that it has suffered a similar fate of cooptation by the corporate forces it presumed to critique. Wellness soon became a niche market for middle-class consumers. The psychologist Lotte Marcus discussed its popularity in a withering 1991 *Mother Jones* article, "Therapy Junkies," that attributed the "cult of wellness" to the punitive culture of conservative "personal responsibility" under Reagan. This is not exactly true, given the concept's origins in post-1960s liberal California, but Marcus's reasoning is understandable, given the way in which wellness's emphasis on one's "responsibility" for their own health dovetailed with a Reaganite use of a moral vocabulary of economic self-reliance. Linking wellness to the then-popular issue of workplace stress, Marcus decried

> telegenic wizards, live seers, and mail-order curanderos ready to ward off whatever phantom villains or microbes may be diagnosed as the root cause of a long-standing complaint, by prescribing a remedial regiment, say, of diet, ritual recantation, positivist thought, the use of **do-it-yourself** improvement kits, and the purging of a variety of "toxins"—social, familial, nutritional, and astral. In this way, sufferers . . . are often condemned to living in perpetual reruns of their roles as victims. As a result, they're sometimes driven to prolong their

pain and anguish, beyond the point where it ought, humanly, to be borne.[3]

Marcus's "mail-order curanderos" are now the online wellness web, hustling vitamin supplements, detox regimens, and all manner of enemas to the sick, underinsured, and vulnerable.

Many private health insurance plans now feature some kind of employer-sponsored wellness program, which combines cash bonuses, prizes, or insurance discounts with gamified nutrition and exercise programs (my own employer offers "wellness bucks" in return for meeting certain benchmarks like quitting smoking, an achievement that would earn me a travel mug). "A company's most precious resource is its employees," writes the celebrity doctor Mehmet Oz in an *Oprah Magazine* article about such programs.[4] Despite the fallacy in this sentence—an oil company's most precious resource, for example, is obviously oil—Oz makes an unintentionally valid point. Employees' health isn't valuable because workers' lives outside the workplace are important—the reason why labor movements struggled for occupational safety standards, socialized medicine, or health insurance in the first place. Rather, wellness matters because employees' health and happiness will minimize their cost to the company and maximize their productivity *at work*.

Harvard Business Review published a study that showed employee wellness programs were, in fact, worth the investment: addressing the bosses who form the magazine's core audience, it concluded that "healthy employees cost you less," by minimizing company health insurance costs. The study concluded that employee wellness programs don't just make employees more inexpensive, but also more loyal, a moral quality hard to measure but impossible to overvalue. Here we circle back to Dunn's original theory that wellness's most lasting benefits are the intangible ones of "spirit." The *HBR* illustrated the theory with an anecdote:

> When MD Anderson initiated its wellness program, president John Mendelsohn took walks throughout the building with wellness **coach** Bill Baun. For many, it was the first time the

president had been in their work space or had shaken their hand, and he tended to start conversations with "How's your wellness?"[5]

In this sense, wellness programs might help the modern firm finally resolve what Dunn, wellness's original prophet, described as the "Western" schism of body and spirit: both now belong to your boss.

ACKNOWLEDGMENTS

Capitalist culture today is not all the acquisition of self, a critic might point out; what about the makerspaces, the teams, the serendipity, the creativity thought to be nurtured by face-to-face contact? One book advises CEOs to model themselves on anthropologists—successful entrepreneurs, after all, must be observant of everyone around them. Be empathetic, others advise; treat everyone as a valued member of a team. "Make everyone feel as though they are a part of the company," advises Bill Parker, the "Innovation Architect" at Quicken Loans, a Detroit mortgage firm whose headquarters are adorned with the bright colors and rec-room entertainments of today's progressive workplaces. Parker's careless phrasing—make employees "feel" as though they are essential parts of the company, whether they actually are or not—is revealing, not only of his motives but of his forebears. It reminds me of Benjamin Franklin, who made a point of pushing his wheelbarrow through the streets of Philadelphia in order to be "esteem'd an industrious, thriving young Man."[1] The *appearance* of industry and success remains as important, if not more so, than the things themselves. This has not changed, even as the names for the values have.

My own experience with this project has routinely given the lie to the entrepreneurial ethic of self-dealing documented in it. Indeed, I have been sustained through this project by the passions for which there is no place in the corporate vocabulary of late capitalism: rage and disgust, passions best shared with others. The project began when I was walking through a downtown Chicago food court with Lara Cohen and Christine Evans, complaining at length about how the word "innovation" seemed to be everywhere. At one point, Christine suggested that instead of just getting mad, I make some small effort at getting even by writing up my criticisms; this turned into a blog chronicling the other terms that celebrated profit and the rule of the market with such guileless enthusiasm. This book is the product of her suggestion. Lara has been the first reader of virtually everything in this book and its most important critic. Nick Fleisher has offered his substantial wit and linguistics expertise, and his advocacy for public education in Scott Walker's Wisconsin has been the source of some of this book's most distressing case studies. Christine has been an advocate for this project beyond that initial conversation, and I have drawn on her insights on the postwar Soviet echoes of our own dreary (but more brightly colored) economism. Sarah Brouillette's support and encouragement has sustained my own commitment to this project, and her work has helped shape it. Leigh Claire La Berge's brilliance and kindness are both without parallel, and I hope this book reflects some of what I have learned from her. Sari Edelstein and Holly Jackson lent vital support at a critical time. Noah Biklen, Beth Blum, Maggie Clinton, Ana Dopico, Greg Grandin, Paul Kershaw, Charley Leary, Tracy Neumann, Kristin Ross, Gustavus Stadler, and Naomi Schiller have been coconspirators, critics, teachers, and supportive friends throughout. Josh Akers, Scout Calvert, Sarika Chandra, Jonathan Flatley, Tara Forbes, David Goldberg, Nora Madden, Emily Movsesian, Aaron Petcoff, and Lisa Ze Winters have listened for the Michigan accents of late-capitalist vocabulary and shared what they've heard with me. Thank you to my Wayne State students for your hopeful example of a generation unimpressed by the promises of an innovation economy. I am endlessly grateful for Jon Miller's example of everyday solidarity, curiosity, and service to others, and for all the help he's given me over the years. What began as a bilious response to the ubiquity of innovation has turned into a long-term project, and for me, it has meant venturing into fields of study far removed from the one I was trained to study. Thanks to Paul Kershaw and Quinn Slobodian for answering my questions about political economy. I'm grateful to my old friend Bruno Díaz, who wrote "Collaboration" with me and who lent his acute critical eye to the strange social world of the twenty-first century consultancy. I have also drawn upon the work, advice, and encouragement of people like Elizabeth Blake, Natalie Cecire, Andrew Friedman, Andrew Goldstone, Mark Healey, Annie McClanahan, Frank Pascuale, Ian Petrie, Ignacio Sánchez-Prado, Keeanga-Yamahtta Taylor, and Audrey Watters. Some of the above I have come to know personally and others I know only through the very social media that produce the commodified entrepreneurial self I describe here, but which are sometimes also good for something. Finally, thanks to Nisha Bolsey, John McDonald, Maya Marshall, and everyone at Haymarket who made this book possible. So, at the risk of committing the sort of sentimentality that might perpetuate the self-dealing ideology of empowerment and sharing this book decries, I am thankful for the community of people who have helped to give this project life. I only hope it retains everyone's exasperation.

INTRODUCTION

1   The influential definition of innovation as the entrepreneurial function is Joseph Schumpeter's, from *Capitalism, Socialism, and Democracy* (London: Routledge, 2003) 132; Thomas Hobbes, *De Cive, or The Citizen* (New York: Appleton-Century-Crofts, 1949) 66; Edmund Burke, *The Beauties of the Late Right Hon. Edmund Burke, Selected from the Writings, &c., of that Extraordinary Man* (London: J.W. Myers, 1798) 316--17.

2   Victor W. Hwang, "The Seven Commandments of Silicon Valley," *Forbes*, September 24, 2012; Thomas Friedman, "Need a Job? Invent It," *New York Times*, March 30, 2013.

3   Raymond Williams, *Keywords: A Vocabulary of Culture and Society* (Oxford: Oxford University Press, 2015), 100.

4   The books inspired by the original *Keywords* share a critical admiration of Williams' work, but also aim to push beyond what Bruce Burgett and Glenn Hendler, editors of *Keywords for American Cultural Studies* (New York: NYU Press, 2007), 4, call Williams' "tendency to assume a narrowly 'British' (largely white, working-class) readership and archive." See Tony Bennett, Lawrence Grossberg, and Meaghan Morris, eds., *New Keywords: A Revised Vocabulary of Culture and Society* (London: Wiley-Blackwell, 2007) and Colin MacCabe, Holly Yanacek, and The Keywords Project, eds., *Keywords for Today: A 21st Century Vocabulary* (New York: Oxford University Press 2018).

5   Luc Boltanski and Eve Chiapello, *The New Spirit of Capitalism,* trans. Gregory Elliott (New York: Verso Books, 2005), 38. The commercial is for American Express: "LIVE LIFE MANIFESTO," accessed June 4, 2018, https://www.youtube.com/watch?v=gh9zC6SUnqY.

6   Valentin Voloshinov, *Marxism and the Philosophy of Language,* trans. Ladislav Matejka and I. R. Titunik (Cambridge, MA: Harvard University Press, 1973), 23.

7   Florina Rodov and Sabrina Truong, "Why Schools Should Teach Entrepreneurship," *Entrepeneur.com,* April 14, 2015; Irene Plagianos, "WeWork is Lauching a Grade School for Budding Entrepreneurs," *Bloomberg.com,* November 6, 2017; David Lidsky, "WeWork Founder Hopes Her New School Will Help 5-Year-Olds Pursue Their Life's Purpose," *Fast Company,* November 6, 2017.

8   Max Weber, *The Protestant Ethic and the Spirit of Capitalism,* trans. Talcott Parsons (London: Routledge Classics, 2001), 16–17.

9   Williams, *Keywords,* xxix, xxxiii.

10   Ernest Mandel, *Late Capitalism,* trans. Joris De Bres (London: Verso Books, 1975), 10, 501; Fredric Jameson, *Postmodernism: or, the Cultural Logic of Late Capitalism* (Durham, NC: Duke University Press, 1995), 36; Annie Lowrey, "Why the Phrase 'Late Capitalism' is Suddenly Everywhere," *The Atlantic,* May 1, 2017.

11   Two critics who object to neoliberalism as a term are Bill Dunn, "Against Neoliberalism as a Concept," *Capital & Class* 41: 3 (2017) 442-444 and Daniel Rodgers, "The Uses and Abuses of 'Neoliberalism,'" *Dissent,* Winter 2018.

12   David Harvey, *A Brief History of Neoliberalism* (New York: Oxford University Pres, 2005), 2; Quinn Slobodian, *Globalists: The End of Empire and the Birth of Neoliberalism* (Cambridge, MA: Harvard University Press, 2018), 12–13, 84–85; Slobodian, "Against the neoliberalism taboo," *FocaalBlog,* January 12, 2018, www.focaalblog.com/2018/01/12/. On right-wing family values and neoliberalism, see Melinda Cooper's *Family Values: Between Noliberalism and the New Social Conservatism* (Brooklyn, NY: Zone Books, 2017).

13   Mandel, *Late Capitalism,* 10–11. On Jameson's rundown of late capitalism's problems as a term, see *Postmodernism,* xviii–xix; Williams, *Keywords,* xxxii. I believe Mike Konczal coined the "latest in capitalism" translation of "late capitalism," in Lowrey, "Why the Phrase 'Late Capitalism' is Suddenly Everwhere."

14   In *Undoing the Demos: Neoliberalism's Stealth Revolution* (Cambridge: Zone Books/MIT Press, 2015), 44, Wendy Brown describes neoliberalism as the "rationality through which capitalism finally swallows humanity."

15   Randy Martin, *The Financialization of Daily Life* (Philadelphia: Temple University Press, 2002) 3; Leigh Claire La Berge and Quinn Slobodian, "Reading for Neoliberalism, Reading like Neoliberals," *American Literary History* 29, no. 3 (2017): 608; Natasha Singer, "Universities Race to Nurture Start-Up Founders of the Future," *New York Times,* December 28, 2015.

16   On the firm as a site of "shared meaning," see Boltanski and Chiapello, *The New Spirit of Capitalism,* 63; Bryan Menegus, "Lyft Thinks It's 'Exciting' That

a Driver Was Working while Giving Birth," *Gizmodo*, September 19, 2016. The entrepreneurial self is a self "sufficient to itself," to paraphrase Sarah Brouillette's argument about the ideal creative worker in *Literature and the Creative Economy* (Palo Alto, CA: Stanford University Press, 2014), 5.

A.

1   Google's ngram data shows "accountability" spiking around the late 1960s; "accountable" has been more consistent over time.

2   US Government Accountability Office, "About GAO," accessed May 16, 2018, www.gao.gov/about/; "GAO's Mission, Responsibilities, Strategies, and Means," accessed May 16, 2018, www.gao.gov/dsp/3mission.html; David Walker, "GAO Answers the Question: What's in a Name?" accessed May 16, 2018, www.gao.gov/about/rollcall07192004.pdf.

3   "Accountability," US Department of Education, September 2, 2003, www2.ed .gov/nclb/accountability/index.html?src=ov.

4   Darren Overfield and Rob Kaiser, "One Out of Every Two Managers is Terrible at Accountability," *Harvard Business Review*, November 9, 2012, https:// hbr.org/2012/11/one-out-of-every-two-managers-is-terrible-at-accountability; "accountability, n." *OED* Online, December 2015. Oxford University Press. All definitions to follow come from the *Oxford English Dictionary*.

5   CGCS Video Maker, "Three-Minute Video Explaining the Common Core State Standards," accessed March 31, 2017, https://vimeo.com/51933492.

6   Anthony Cody, "Can California Offer a New Model for Accountability? Or Are We Still Chasing Test Scores?" *Education Week*, June 7, 2014.

7   Alex Vitale, "Police and the Liberal Fantasy," *Jacobin,* October 19, 2017, www.jacobinmag.com/2017/10/police-reform-prisons-racism-vitale.

8   Leon Trotsky, *Our Revolution* [1907], trans. Anya Bostock, accessed November 28, 2017, www.marxists.org/archive/trotsky/1907/1905/ch02.htm; James Fink, *The Automotive Age* (Cambridge, MA: MIT Press, 1990), 48; E. P. Thompson, *The Making of the English Working Class* (London: Penguin Books, 1980), 12.

9   Williams, *Keywords*, 10.

10 Randle Cotgrave, *A Dictionarie of the French and English Tongues* (London: Adam Islip, 1611), n.p. The *OED* uses this aphorism in its entry for "artisan." William Morris, "Artists and Artisan as an Artist Sees It," *Commonweal* 3, no. 87, September 10, 1887, republished at www.marxists.org/archive/morris /works/1887/commonweal/09-artist-artisan.htm; Williams, *Keywords*, 10.

11 Susan Heller Anderson, "Making Chocolates in the Artisan's Way," *New York Times*, December 17, 1980; Patricia Wells, "Vive la Baguette: As French as Paris," *New York Times,* October 9, 1983; Amanda Hesser, "A Revolutionary Idea: Trading Grape for Apple," *New York Times*, November 14, 2001.

12   T. J. Jackson Lears, *No Place of Grace: Antimodernism and the Transformation of American Culture, 1880–1922* (Chicago: University of Chicago Press, 1981) 60–65.

B.

1   Robert Camp, *Benchmarking: The Search for Industry Best Practices that Lead to Superior Performance* (Milwaukee, WI: ASQ Quality Press, 1989), xi, 13, 3.
2   Brown, *Undoing the Demos*, 138–40; "About Us," Entangled Solutions, accessed November 30, 2017, www.entangled.solutions/about/.
3   "Politics 345: Political Marketing," The University of Auckland, accessed April 4, 2017, https://flexiblelearning.auckland.ac.nz/political_marketing/24.html; "Excerpts from Addresses by Keynote Speakers at Democratic Convention," *New York Times,* July 14, 1992; Joseph P. Williams, "Last Call: GOP Leadership Says They Want Outreach, but Selma's a Bridge Too Far," *US News and World Report,* March 6, 2015.
4   Tom Peters, "The Brand Called You," *Fast Company,* August 31, 1997; Naomi Klein, *No Logo: Taking Aim at the Brand Bullies* (Toronto: Knopf Canada, 2009), 21.
5   Daniel Lair, Katie Sullivan, and George Cheney, "Marketization and the Recasting of the Professional Self: The Rhetoric and Ethics of Personal Branding," *Management Communication Quarterly* 18 (2005), 307–43.
6   Michael Beverland, in *Building Brand Authenticity: 7 Habits of Iconic Brands* (New York: Palgrave McMillan, 2009), 2, writes that "marketers need to imbue their brands with a warts and all humanity and use the tools at their disposal to tell, and help others tell, stories."
7   Brouillette, *Literature and the Creative Economy,* 24.

C.

1   Nancy McLean, *Democracy in Chains* (New York: Penguin Books, 2017), 80.
2   Julian Betts and Tom Loveless, "School Choice, Equity, and Efficiency," in Betts and Loveless, eds., *Getting Choice Right: Ensuring Equity and Efficiency in Education Policy* (Washington, DC: Brookings Institution Press, 2005), 3–4; "Schools of Choice," Michigan Department of Education, accessed November 2, 2017, www.michigan.gov/mde/0,4615,7-140-81351_81352_81356---,00.html. Betsy DeVos, Secretary of Education under President Trump, identifies "choice" with "empowerment" in "President Trump delivers on education promises," *USA Today,* March 2, 2017.
3   Margaret Thatcher, "The New Renaissance," March 14, 1977, www.margaretthatcher.org/document/103336. "Economic freedom is an essential requisite for political freedom," write Milton and Rose Friedman in their 1980 polemic *Free to Choose: A Personal Statement* (New York: Harcourt Brace Jovanovich, 1980), 3.

4   On Thatcher's Zurich speech, see Philip Mirowski, *Never Let a Serious Crisis Go to Waste: How Neoliberalism Survived the Financial Meltdown* (New York: Verso Books, 2013), 95.

5   Andrea J. Lee, ed., "Thomas Leonard: 10 Years Later (1955–2003)," accessed December 2, 2017, http://bestofthomas.com/docs/thomas-leonard-full.pdf; Eve Tahmincioglu, "Coaches Wanted In the Game Of Life," *New York Times*, January 13, 2008; Kate Stone Lombardi, "Exploring the Secrets of the Hidden Box," *New York Times*, May 30, 2004.

6   Thomas J. Leonard, *The 28 Laws of Attraction: Stop Chasing Success and Let it Chase You* (New York: Simon and Schuster, 2007), 13.

7   Jenny Lyn Bader, "Relying on the Competence Of Strangers," *The New York Times*, April 1, 1999; Marilyn Kochman, "Coach or Couch, Choose Your Therapy," July 13, 2003; Tahmincioglu, "Coaches Wanted In the Game Of Life."

8   Russell H. Conwell, *Acres of Diamonds* (New York: Harper & Brothers, 1915), 3–18; Abraham Maslow, "A Theory of Human Motivation," *Psychological Review* 50, no. 4 (1943): 382.

9   The International Coach Federation reports that the majority of women come to coaches to improve "work/life balance," while men solicited coaching to expand their professional opportunities. Men were slightly more likely than women to receive coaching, according to the 2014 report (International Coach Federation, "New ICF Research Offers Inside Look at Coaching Consumers," May 20, 2014, www.coachfederation.org). Some news reports, like Taffy Brodesser-Akner's "The Merchant of Just Be Happy," *New York Times*, December 28, 2013, claim that women are the primary consumers of coaching overall.

10   Ashley Stahl, "Should You Hire A Life Coach?" *Forbes*, September 23, 2015.

11   Philip Evans and Bob World, "Collaboration Rules," *Harvard Business Review* 83, no. 7/8 (July/August 2005): 96–104.

12   Target recruitment video, accessed January 10, 2018, www.dailymotion.com /video/x35gl6i.

13   Will Knight, "How Human-Robot Teamwork Will Upend Manufacturing," *MIT Technology Review*, September 16, 2014; Jacob Morgan, "Why the Collaborative Economy is Changing Everything," *Forbes,* October 16, 2014; On "co-creation," see Sam Milbrath, "Co-creation: 5 examples of brands driving customer-driven innovation," *Vision Critical*, August 5, 2016, www.visioncritical .com/5-examples-how-brands-are-using-co-creation/.

14   Karl Marx, *Capital: A Critique of Political Economy*, vol. 1. trans. Ernest Mandel (New York: Penguin Books, 1990), 443.

15   Remley Glass, "Gentlemen, the Corn Belt!" *Harper's Magazine*, July 1933, 202; Gene Currivan, "8-Hour High School Day Urged to Permit Graduation in 2 Years," *New York Times*, October 3, 1963; Centre for Educational Research

and Innovation, *Information Technologies and Basic Learning: Reading, Writing, Science and Mathematics* (Paris: Organization for Economic Co-operation and Development, 1987), 170. On competency-based higher education, see the US Department of Education's definition at "Competency-Based Learning or Personalized Learning," accessed June 18, 2018, www.ed.gov/oii-news /competency-based-learning-or-personalized-learning; "UW Flexible Option," accessed November 4, 2017, https://flex.wisconsin.edu/ (italics mine).

16 "Electronics Specialist Competency Profile," The University of North Carolina Wilmington, accessed March 28. 2017, http://uncw.edu/hr/documents /ElectronicsSpecialistProfile.pdf.

17 Sarah Beckett, "What's the Difference Between Skills and Competencies?" accessed January 12, 2016, www.hrsg.ca/whats-the-difference-between-skills -and-competencies.

18 "Skills or Competencies...What's the Difference?" HRTMS, April 4, 2016. www.hrtms.com/blog/skills-or-competencieswhats-the-difference.

19 C.K. Prahalad and Gary Hamel, "The Core Competence of the Corporation," *Harvard Business Review*, May–June 1990, 4; "Core competence," *Economist*, September 15, 2008, www.economist.com/node/12231124

20 Ibid., 14.

21 Carla Rapaport, "Charles Handy Sees the Future, *Fortune*, October 31, 1994 http://archive.fortune.com/magazines/fortune/fortune_archive/1994 /10/31/79894/index.htm.

22 Joseph Jaffe, *Join the Conversation: How to Engage Marketing-Weary Consumers with the Power of Community, Dialogue, and Partnership* (Hoboken, N.J.: John Wiley & Sons, 2007).

23 In announcing the Initiative, Clinton resolved to lead "the American people in a great and unprecedented conversation on race." Cited in Ibram Kendi, *Stamped from the Beginning: The Definitive History of Racist Ideas in America* (New York: PublicAffairs, 2016), 467. See the archived website of the President's Initiative on Race, accessed April 3, 2017, https://clinton3.nara.gov/Initiatives/OneAmerica/america.html.

24 Glenn C. Loury's "Why Talk About Race: Welfare and Crime Demand More Than Feel-Good Chat," *The Washington Post*, December 7, 1997 is a forceful critique of the therapeutic model Clinton employed; Michael P. Jeffries, *Paint the White House Black: Barack Obama and the Meaning of Race in America* (Palo Alto, CA: Stanford University Press, 2013) 181.

25 Jonathan Capehart, "That honest conversation about race everyone wants? We can't handle it," *The Washington Post,* March 2, 2014; Clarissa Hayward, "It takes more than a 'National Conversation About Race' to change racial injustice," *Cleveland.com*, February 9, 2014; Rich Lowry, "Conversation About Race? Get Real," *Politico*, July 7, 2013. The piece by Lowry is a right-wing

critique of the consensus model of the conversation that focused on "Black criminality."

26   Craig Erwich, "Hulu at the 2014 Television Critics Association Summer Press Tour," July 12, 2014, http://blog.hulu.com/2014/07/12/hulu-at-the-2014 -television-critics-association-summer-press-tour/.

27   Karl Marx, *Capital*, trans. Ben Fowkes (New York: Vintage Books, 1977), 166.

28   Benjamin Hart, "'Breaking Bad' isn't content! Why we need to stop using this terrible noun," *Salon,* May 22, 2014.

29   Daniel Okrent, "AOL–Time Warner Merger: Happily Ever After?," *Time Asia,* January 24, 2000, www.cnn.com/ASIANOW/time/magazine/2000/0124/cover1 .html.

30   Mark Davies, *The Corpus of Historical American English (COHA): 400 million words, 1810–2009*, https://corpus.byu.edu/coha/; "Content," accessed April 5, 2017, www.merriam-webster.com/dictionary/content.

31   Corbin Hair, "Writers Explain What It's Like Toiling on the Content Farm," *Mediashift*, July 21, 2010; Nicholas Spanger, "In Demand: A Week Inside the Future of Journalism," *Columbia Journalism Review*, November/December 2010.

32   California State Department of Education, "California Common Core State Standards" (2013), 2.

33   Williams quotes Augustine's dictum in his entry on "creative" in *Keywords,* 45. See Michael North's account of creation and renewal in early Christianity in *Novelty: A History of the New* (Chicago: University of Chicago Press, 2013), 36–43.

34   Williams, *Keywords,* 46.

35   In the *OED*'s definition of "creativity," the earliest example of the noun comes from Adolphus Ward, *A History of English Dramatic Literature to the Death of Queen Anne*, vol. I (London: Macmillan and Co., 1875), 506. Ward was a Shakespeare critic who wrote of the "spontaneous flow of his poetic creativity." On "creativity" and its separation from divine "creation," see Rob Pope, *Creativity: History, Theory, Practice* (London: Routledge, 2005), 16–21.

36   Cindi Katz, *Growing Up Global: Economic Restructuring and Children's Everyday Lives* (Minneapolis: University of Minnesota Press, 2004), x, defines social reproduction as "that broad range of practices and social relations that maintain and reproduce particular relations of production along with the material social grounds in which they take place. It is as much the fleshy, messy, and indeterminate stuff of everyday life as it is a set of structured practices that unfold in dialectical relation to production, with which it is mutually constitutive and in tension."

37   Samuel Bacharach, in "Why Art is Good for Entrepreneurs," calls museums "monuments to entrepreneurship." A related version of this argument sees the businessperson's instincts as basically artistic and imaginative. Grant

Cardone, "10 Things the Artist and the Entrepreneur Have in Common," *Entrepreneur*, February 9, 2017.

38 Karl Marx and Friedrich Engels, *Manifesto of the Communist Party*, trans. Samuel Moore with Friedrich Engels, accessed March 1, 2018, www.marxists.org /archive/marx/works/1848/communist-manifesto/ch01.htm; Schumpeter, *Capitalism, Socialism, and Democracy*, 83.

39 Brouillette, *Literature and the Creative Economy*, 7; Richard Florida, *The Rise of the Creative Class* (New York: Basic Books, 2012) 248–49. On the Cold War politics of 1950s psychological theories of creativity, see Pope, *Creativity*, 19–20. On the compatibility of iconoclastic modernism and the geopolitical aims of the United States, see Frances Stonor Saunders's *The Cultural Cold War: The CIA and the World of Arts and Letters* (New York: The New Press, 2013).

40 *Florida, Rise of the Creative Class*, xi, 8, 15, 23.

41 Brouillette, *Literature and the Creative Economy*, 2–3; 38–39.

42 Gustavus Stadler, *Troubling Minds: The Cultural Politics of Genius in the United States, 1840–1890* (Minneapolis: University of Minnesota Press, 2006), xiv.

43 Jason Gregory, "Metallica, Slipknot Curate New Judas Priest Album 'The Chosen One,'" *Gigwise,* September 15, 2011, www.gigwise.com; "Duo Set Out to Curate Ultimate Drinking Experiences with Matte&Gloss," *Capitol Hill Seattle Blog*, February 2, 2014, www.capitolhillseattle.com/2014/02/capitol-hill-fooddrink -duo-set-out-to-curate-ultimate-drinking-experiences-with-mattegloss/; "Worth Magazine Launches Curator Luxury Showcase During Art Basel Week," November 26, 2013, http://sandow.com; "About Us," www.eventsdirect. co.nz/about-us, accessed December 10, 2015; "The New Luxury: The Curated Wardrobe," *Fashionising*, accessed December 10, 2015, www.fashionising.com /clothing/b--curated-wardrobe-6616.html. Alex Williams, "On the Tip of Creative Tongues," *New York Times*, October 2, 2009.

44 "Frequently Asked Questions About Data Curation," Digital Humanities Data Curation, accessed December 10, 2015, http://guide.dhcuration.org/ faq/; John Hoerr, *We Can't Eat Prestige: The Women Who Organized Harvard* (Philadelphia: Temple University Press, 1997).

45 Stephanie Tilenius, "The New Curated Consumer Marketplace Model: 10 Criteria For Success," *Forbes*, October 3, 2013. Tilenius's title, according to her author bio, is "entrepreneur in residence at Kleiner Perkins Caufield & Byers," another example of the private sector rhetorically borrowing from the art world.

46 David Levi Strauss, *From Head to Hand: Art and the Manual* (New York: Oxford University Press, 2010), 149.

47 Meg Carter, "How 'Content Curators' are Connecting Consumers," *The Guardian*, October 20, 2011.

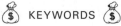

D.

1   Steve Lohr, "The Age of Big Data," *New York Times*, February 11, 2012; John Markoff, "Government Aims to Build A 'Data Eye In the Sky,'" *New York Times,* October 11, 2011. For a skeptical appraisal, see Siva Vaidhyanathan, *The Googlization of Everything (And Why We Should Worry)* (Berkeley: University of California Press, 2011).

2   Doug Laney, "3D Data Management: Controlling Data Volume, Velocity, and Variety," *Application Delivery Strategies*, Meta Group, February 6, 2001; Frank Pasquale, *The Black Box Society: The Secret Algorithms That Control Money and Information* (Cambridge, MA: Harvard University Press, 2015), 3.

3   Tim Brown & Jocelyn Wyatt, "Design Thinking for Social Innovation," *Stanford Social Innovation Review*, Winter 2010.

4   "A place for explorers and experimenters at Stanford University," Stanford d.school, accessed May 24, 2018, https://dschool.stanford.edu/about/. On design thinking in prisons, see "Design Thinking for Prison Industries: Exchanging design tools, methods and processes with prisons in London and Ahmedabad to build inmate resilience," *UK Research and Innovation*, http://gtr.ukri.org/projects?ref=AH%2FM005666%2F1; Rikha Sharma Rani, "New Zealand Tries a Different Kind of Private Prison," *CityLab*, August 31, 2017.

5   Lilly Irani, "'Design Thinking': Defending Silicon Valley at the Apex of Global Labor Hierarchies," *Catalyst: Feminism, Theory, Technoscience* 4 (2018), 3–6.

6   Two examples: Taz Loomans, "8 Toilet Designs That Could Save Millions of Lives Around the World," January 3, 2015, https://inhabitat.com/8-toilet-designs-that-could-save-millions-of-lives-around-the-world/; "Reinvent the Toilet Challenge: Strategy Overview," Bill & Melinda Gates Foundation, accessed January 20, 2018, www.gatesfoundation.org/What-We-Do/Global-Growth-and-Opportunity/Water-Sanitation-and-Hygiene/Reinvent-the-Toilet-Challenge.

7   IDEO *Design Thinking for Educators Toolkit*, 2012,16. The advice comes under the heading, "Problems are just opportunities for design in disguise"; Megan Erickson, *Class War: The Privatization of Childhood* (New York: Verso Books, 2015), 113–14.

8   Justin Fox, "The Disruption Myth," *The Atlantic,* October 2014, www.theatlantic.com/magazine/archive/2014/10/the-disruption-myth/379348/; Andy Rachleff, "What 'Disrupt' Really Means," *TechCrunch,* February 16, 2013, https://techcrunch.com/2013/02/16/the-truth-about-disruption/.

9   See James Spence, *The American Union; Its Effect on National Character and Policy, with an Inquiry into Secession as a Constitutional Right and the Causes of the Disruption* (London: Richard Bentley, 1862), 92.

10   Clayton M. Christensen, *The Innovator's Dilemma: When New Technologies Cause Great Firms to Fail* (Boston: Harvard Business School Press, 1997), xvi–xvii;

Clayton M. Christensen and Michael E. Raynor, *The Innovator's Solution: Creating and Sustaining Successful Growth* (Boston: Harvard Business School Press, 2003), 43–49.

11 Richard Foster used the term "technological discontinuities" in his 1986 book *Innovation: The Attacker's Advantage* (New York: Summit Books, 1986) and told the *Atlantic*, "I will forever rue the day I didn't call it 'disruption'" (Fox, "The Disruption Myth"). What Christensen called "disruptive innovation" also resembles what others have called "radical" or "drastic" innovation. See Kenneth Arrow, "Economic Welfare and the Allocation of Resources to Invention," *The Rate and Direction of Economic Activity*, ed., R. R. Nelson (Princeton: Princeton University Press, 1962); Rebecca M. Henderson, "Underinvestment and Incompetence as Responses to Radical Innovation: Evidence from the Photolithographic Alignment Industry," *The RAND Journal of Economics* 24, no. 2 (Summer 1993): 248–70.

12 Andrew A. King and Baljir Baatartogtokh, "How Useful Is the Theory of Disruptive Innovation?" *Sloane Management Review* (Fall 2015).

13 Jill Lepore, "The Disruption Machine," *The New Yorker*, June 23, 2014.

14 Schumpeter, *Capitalism, Socialism, and Democracy*, 84; Christensen and Raynor, *The Innovator's Solution*, 285.

15 Christensen and Raynor, *The Innovator's Solution*, 17, 34; Shelly Dutton, "Navy SEAL Leadership Secrets that Help You Win on the Digital Disruption Battlefield," *Digitalist*, June 1, 2016, accessed October 13, 2017, www.digitalistmag.com/future-of-work/2016/06/01/navy-seal-leadership-secrets-win-on-digital-disruption-battlefield-04244938.

16 Janet L. Yellen, "The Financial Markets, Housing, and the Economy," The Federal Reserve Bank of San Francisco Economic Letter, April 18, 2008, www.frbsf.org/economic-research/publications/economic-letter/2008/april/financial-markets-housing-economy/.

17 Grant McCracken, "The Five Stages of Disruption Denial," *Harvard Business Review*, April 15, 2013.

18 Steven Gelber, "Do-It-Yourself: Constructing, Repairing and Maintaining Domestic Masculinity," *American Quarterly* 49, no. 1 (1997): 67.

19 Teal Triggs, "Scissors and Glue: Punk Fanzines and the Creation of a DIY Aesthetic," *Journal of Design History* 19, no. 1 (2006): 69–83.

20 Lane Relyea, *Your Everyday Art World* (Cambridge, MA: The MIT Press, 2013), 5.

21 Examples are legion: see the website www.diygenius.com/diy-education, which links to various services and offers advice for the "self-educator."

E.

1 Linda Wechsler, "Building Portland's Maker Ecosystem," Oregon Manufacturing Extension Partnership, November 23, 2015, www.omep.org/

building-portlands-maker-ecosystem-a-new-local-partnership-aims-to-help-makers-succeed; "Innovation Ecosystem," Georgia Institute of Technology, www.gatech.edu/innovation-ecosystem; Bruce Katz and Julie Wagner, "The Rise of Innovation Districts: A New Geography of Innovation in America," *Metropolitan Policy Program at Brookings*, May 2014, 2; Margaret C. Brindle and Peter N. Stearns, *Facing Up to Management Faddism: A New Look at an Old Force* (Westport, CT: Quorum Books, 2001), 16.

2   Michelle Murphy, *Sick Building Syndrome and the Problem of Uncertainty: Environmental Politics Tecnoscience, and Women Workers* (Durham, NC: Duke University Press, 2006) 19. For the nineteenth-century dream of outdoor climate control, see Charles Asbury Stephens's *Natural Salvation, Immortal Life on the Earth from the Growth of Knowledge and the Development of the Human Brain* (Norway Lake, MN: The Laboratory, 1903), 236.

3   Murphy sketches the history of organizational ecology in *Sick Building Syndrome,* 132–41. Population and organizational ecology is attributed to Michael T. Hannan and John Freeman's "The Population Ecology of Organization, *American Journal of Sociology* 82, no. 5 (1977): 929–64.

4   James F. Moore, "Predators and Prey: A New Ecology of Competition," *Harvard Business Review,* May-June 1993. Moore ends his article with the slogan "only the fittest survive," a reference not to Darwin, as he seems to think, but to Herbert Spencer, a fitting irony, given Spencer's use of a loose scientific analogy to justify the class hierarchy of his day.

5   Williams, *Keywords,* 110.

6   Christensen, *The Innovator's Dilemma*, xix.

7   Shirley Ann Jackson, "Remarks at the Detroit Economic Club: Expediting Serendipity: Building an Innovation Ecosystem," October 2009, http://president.rpi.edu/speeches/2009/expediting-serendipity-building-innovation-ecosystem.

8   Deborah J. Jackson, "What is an Innovation Ecosystem?" National Science Foundation, 2011, accessed December 5, 2017, http://erc-assoc.org/sites/default/files/topics/policy_studies/DJackson_Innovation%20Ecosystem_03-15-11.pdf; 4; Deog-Seong Oh, Fred Phillips, Sehee Park, Eunghyun Lee, "Innovation ecosystems: A critical examination," *Technovation* 54 (2016) www.sciencedirect.com/science/article/pii/S0166497216300062#bib15.

9   Jackson, "What is an Innovation Ecosystem?" 8.

10   Anne-Emmanuèle Calvès, "Empowerment: The History of a Key Concept in Contemporary Development Discourse," trans. JPD Systems, *Revue Tiers Monde* 4 no. 200 (2009), i–ix.

11   Paolo Freire, *The Pedagogy of the Oppressed,* trans. Myra Bergman Ramos (New York: Bloomsbury, 2014), 166–67; "Cultural Action and Concientization," in *The Politics of Education: Culture, Power, and Liberation,* trans. Donald Macedo (Westport, CT: Bergin and Garvey, 1985), 69–70. Barbara Bryant Solomon,

Black Empowerment: Social Work in Oppressed Communities (New York: Columbia University Press, 1976), 16–26.

12   OECD-DAC, "Aid in Support of Women's Economic Empowerment," January 2011, www.oecd.org/dac/gender-development/aid-women-economic-empowerment.htm.

13   Jia Tolentino, "How 'Empowerment' Became Something for Women to Buy," *New York Times,* April 12, 2016.

14   Philip Vasallo, "Empowering Parents Through School Choice," *The Cato Institute,* October 20, 2000, www.cato.org/publications/commentary/empowering-parents-through-school-choice; Sarah Lenhoff, "Yes, Michigan's schools are failing. But don't blame it on parents," *Bridge,* October 24, 2017.

15   Stokely Carmichael, "What We Want," *New York Review of Books,* September 22, 1966, www.nybooks.com/articles/1966/09/22/what-we-want/.

16   Robert Putnam, *Bowling Alone: The Collapse and Revival of American Community* (New York: Simon and Schuster, 2001), 18–20.

17   *Letters Written by the Earl of Chesterfield to His Son* (Philadelphia: J.B. Lippincott, 1876), 372.

18   Joshua Akers, "Emerging Market City," *Environment and Planning A: Economy and Space* 47, no. 9 (2015) 1851.

19   Detroit Future City, "Civic Engagement: Supporting Lasting Civic Capacity in Detroit," 2012, 694, https://detroitfuturecity.com/wp-content/uploads/2017/07/DFC_CivicEngagement_2nd.pdf.

20   Marx and Engels, *Manifesto of the Communist Party,* accessed May 24, 2018, www.marxists.org/archive/marx/works/1848/communist-manifesto/ch01.htm; Joseph Schumpeter, *The Theory of Economic Development* (Cambridge, MA: Harvard University Press, 1934), 74; Schumpeter, *Capitalism, Socialism, and Democracy,* 132.

21   E. P. Thompson, *The Making of the English Working Class* (New York: Pantheon Books, 1964), 778; "An Open Letter to Leszek Kolakowski," *Socialist Register,* 1973, www.marxists.org/archive/thompson-ep/1973/kolakowski.htm.

22   Paul Sweezy, "Professor Schumpeter's Theory of Innovation," *The Review of Economics and Statistics* 25, no. 1 (1943): 96.

23   Tobias Kollner, *Practising Without Belonging?: Entrepreneurship, Morality, and Religion in Contemporary Russia* (Zurich: LIT Verlag Münster, 2013), 32.

24   Weber, *The Protestant Ethic and the Spirit of Capitalism,* 51.

25   Colleen DeBaise, "How to Decide if Entrepreneurship is Right For You," *Wall Street Journal,* accessed December 10, 2015, http://guides.wsj.com/small-business/starting-a-business/how-to-decide-if-entrepreneurship-is-right-for-you.

26   *CBS Evening News with Scott Pelley,* March 26, 2012; "Richard Branson: The P.T. Barnum of British Business," *Entrepreneur,* October 10, 2008. This comparison is meant to be complimentary, with no suggestions of the fraudulence for which

Barnum was well known; "What is a Social Entrepreneur?" accessed December 10, 2015, www.schwabfound.org/content/what-social-entrepreneur.

27 "About Us," *Virgin Group,* accessed December 10, 2015, www.virgin.com/about -us; Charlie Wells, "Teaching Children How to Be Entrepreneurs," *Wall Street Journal,* April 8, 2014; "Life and Career Skills," *SuperCamp,* www.supercamp.com /life-and-career-skills.aspx#AboutTab3, accessed December 10, 2015; Chris Quintana, "The Most Cringeworthy Monuments to Colleges' Innovation Jargon," *Chronicle of Higher Ed,* March 6, 2017.

28 The National Commission on Excellence in Education, "A Nation At Risk," April 1983, www2.ed.gov/pubs/NatAtRisk/risk.html.

29 Bill Readings, *The University in Ruins* (Cambridge: Harvard University Press, 1996), 39.

30 Kathyn L. Allan, "Excellence: A New Keyword for Education?" *Critical Quarterly* 49, no. 1 (2007): 59.

31 Readings, *University in Ruins,* 24–27.

F.

1 Stewart Thornhill, "Out of Failure Springs Innovation," *Financial Times,* April 6, 2014; Adam Davidson, "Welcome to the Failure Age!" *New York Times,* November 12, 2014.

2 Paul Schoemaker, "Why Failure is the Foundation of Innovation," *Inc.,* August 13, 2012; Baba Shiv, "Why Failure Drives Innovation," *Insights by Stanford Business,* March 1, 2011, www.gsb.stanford.edu/insights/baba-shiv-why-failure -drives-innovation. At Oakland's Redwood Day school, "students learn about Design Thinking where one's 'failures' are ultimately one's greatest opportunities," "Kindergarten," Redwood Day, accessed February 20, 2018, www.rdschool .org/page/program/curriculum/kindergarten.

3 Jane Porter, "How Failure Made These Entrepreneurs Millions," *Entrepreneur,* June 14, 2013.

4 See, for example, R. Boyer, *The Search for Labour Market Flexibility: The European Economies in Transition* (Oxford: Clarendon Press, 1988); for an overview of the literature on labor market flexibility, see Jamie Peck, *Work-place: The Social Regulation of Labor Markets* (New York: The Guilford Press, 1996), 141.

5 The plural counting noun "flexibilities" is not itself new. But it has never been common and was formerly used to describe an attribute of singers or musicians—the dexterity, according to the *OED,* "of the voice or fingers."

6 "Governor Walker Signs Legislation to Preserve Natural Resources," March 23, 2012, https://walker.wi.gov/press-releases/governor-walker-signs-legis- lation-preserve-natural-resources; On flexibilities in Wisconsin public higher education, see Angela Chen, "Online Degree Program Lets Students Test Out of What They Already Know," *The Chronicle of Higher Education,* Wired

Campus Blog, June 20, 2012; "Flex Your Potential," *UW Flexible Option: University of Wisconsin System*, accessed December 12, 2015, http://flex.wisconsin. edu.

7   As Bryce Covert writes, the progressive sheen of such policies conceals the inequality of their application: some firms, for example, only offer "flexible scheduling" to new mothers in white-collar positions. "The Danger of Policies That Take Mothers Out of the Office," *The Nation*, March 13, 2015.

8   Stephanie Luce and Naoki Fujita, "Discounted Jobs: How Retailers Sell Workers Short," Retail Action Project and the Murphy Institute for Worker Education and Labor Studies, March 1, 2012, 12.

9   "Annual Message to Congress," December 5, 1861, in Roy P. Basler, ed., *The Collected Works of Abraham Lincoln*, vol. 5 (New Brunswick: Rutgers University Press, 1953), 52.

10   Editorial, "Reconversion to What?" *Life*, August 28, 1944; Milton Friedman, *Capitalism and Freedom* (Chicago: The University of Chicago Press, 2002), 10–11.

G.

1   Angela Duckworth, Chris Peterson, Michael D. Matthews, and Dennis R. Kelly, "Grit: Perseverance and Passion for Long-Term Goals," *Journal of Personality and Social Psychology* 92, no. 6 (2007), 1087–88. "Focus on Character," kipp, accessed February 23, 2018, www.kipp.org/approach/character/.

2   Ethan W. Ris, "Grit: A Short History of a Useful Concept," *Journal of Educational Controversy* 10, no. 1 (2015): 4–5; Horatio Alger, Jr. *Grit, Or the Young Boatman of Pine Point* (New York: Hurst & Company, n.d.), 3.

3   Melissa Dahl, "Don't Believe the Hype About Grit, Pleads the Scientist Behind the Concept," *The Cut*, May 9, 2016.

4   Ris, "Grit," 7.

5   On the nineteenth-century virtues of thrift, sobriety, and industry, see Joel Schwartz, *Fighting Poverty with Virtue: Moral Reform and America's Urban Poor, 1825–2000* (Bloomington: University of Indiana Press, 2000).

6   Duckworth, *Grit*, 216.

7   "Those who defy the odds" to graduate from community college, Duckworth writes at one point, "are especially gritty." Elsewhere, she observes how the Seattle Seahawks, who have adopted grit as a team philosophy, "defied the odds" to advance to the Super Bowl in consecutive years. Duckworth, *Grit*, 11, 263.

H.

1   Peter R. Samson, "Annotated First Edition of the TMRC Dictionary (1959)," accessed March 10, 2017, www.gricer.com/tmrc/dictionary1959.html; Gina

Trapani, *Lifehacker: 88 Tech Tricks to Turbocharge Your Day* (New York: John Wiley & Sons, 2007), xxiii.

2 Ben Yagoda, "A Short History of Hack," *The New Yorker,* March 6, 2014.

3 "The World of Data Confronts the Joy of Hacking, *New York Times*, August 18, 1983; Cory Doctorow, "Notes from Danny O'Brien's NotCon Recap of Life Hacks," www.craphound.com/lifehacks2.txt, June 6, 2004.

4 Kim Zetter and Kevin Poulsen, "'I Can't Believe What I'm Confessing to You': The Wikileaks Chats," *Wired*, June 10, 2010; Chuck Gomez, "The Hacker Wars Hits NYC, *The Huffington Post,* October 15, 2014.

5 Adrian Chen, "A So-Called Expert's Uneasy Dive into the Trump-Russia Frenzy," *The New Yorker,* February 22, 2018; Jameson, *Postmodernism,* 34.

6 Nikil Saval, "The Secret History of Life-Hacking," *Pacific Standard*, April 22, 2014; Frederick Winslow Taylor, *The Principles of Scientific Management* (1911) www.marxists.org/reference/subject/economics/taylor/principles/ch01.htm.

7 Gina Trapani, "Interview: father of 'life hacks' Danny O'Brien," March 17, 2005, https://lifehacker.com/036370/interview-father-of-life-hacks-danny-obrien.

8 See Jennifer Rubin, a "center-right" columnist, on the "human capital" deficit in "Hillary's Toughest Question," *Washington Post*, September 26, 2016; Christian González-Rivera, analyst at the Center for an Urban Future, a nonpartisan think tank, in "Trump wants to be a jobs president, so he can't ignore human capital," *The Hill*, May 3, 2017; "The Global Human Capital Report, 2017: Preparing People for the Future of Work," World Economic Forum, 2017, in which the Forum explains this figure by explaining that "nations are neglecting or wasting, on average, 38% of their talent"; "50,000 Vegas Casino Workers to Vote on Strike Over Contract," *New York Times*, May 9, 2018.

9 Theodore W. Schultz, "Investment in Human Capital," *The American Economic Review* 51, no. 1 (1961): 2, 14.

10 Gary Becker, *Human Capital: A Theoretical and Empirical Analysis with Special Reference to Education* (New York: National Bureau of Economic Research, 1975), 9. Becker defines "investments in human capital" as "activities that influence future monetary and psychic income by increasing the resources in people." By "habits," he means things like punctuality and a propensity to smoke. See "Human Capital," *The Concise Encyclopedia of Economics,* Library of Economics and Liberty (1993), accessed February 5, 2018, www.econlib.org /library/Enc1/HumanCapital.html.

11 Barack Obama, "Remarks by President Obama at the Global Entrepreneurship Summit," Nairobi, Kenya, July 25, 2015, https://obamawhitehouse. archives.gov/the-press-office/2015/07/25/remarks-president-obama-global-entrepreneurship-summit; "An Interview with the President," *The Economist,* August 2, 2014.

12   Lester Spence, *Knocking the Hustle: Against the Neoliberal Turn in Black Politics* (Brooklyn: Punctum Books, 2015), 9.

13   Samuel Bowles and Herbert Gintis, "The Problem with Human Capital Theory—a Marxian Critique," *The American Economic Review* 65, no. 2 (1975): 82. In his reading of human capital's displacement of labor as a category of analysis, Foucault emphasized that human capital treated as economic assets certain acquired traits as well as "genetic" elements. "If you want a child whose human capital, understood simply in terms of innate and hereditary elements, is high," Foucault proposed, then you will seek a spouse likely to help: a "co-producer of this future human capital, someone who has significant human capital themselves." *The Birth of Biopolitics: Lectures at the Collège de France, 1978–79*, trans. Graham Burchell (New York: Palgrave Macmillan, 2008), 228.

I.

1   "America's Best Society Dancer Invents a 'Decent' Tango—The 'Innovation,'" *The Day Book*, January 31, 1914; "Dancing the 'No-Touch,'" *The Omaha Bee*, February 18, 1914.

2   Benoît Godin, *Innovation Contested: The Idea of Innovation Over the Centuries* (New York: Routledge, 2015), 5, 11. For example, Emma Goldman referred proudly to anarchism as "the most revolutionary and uncompromising innovator" in 1910. Goldman, "Anarchism: What it Really Stands For," *Marxists Internet Archive,* accessed July 26, 2018, www.marxists.org/reference/archive/goldman/works/1910s/anarchism.htm.

3   Schumpeter, *Theory of Economic Development*, 88–89; *Capitalism, Socialism, and Democracy* (London: Routledge, 2003), 132; "Gimbels—The Store of a Million Gifts!" *New York Tribune,* December 5, 1915.

4   Hobbes, *De Cive*, 66.

5   Regan McMahon, "Samuel Barondes Book on Assessing Personalities," *San Francisco Chronicle*, July 18, 2011; Steve Raabe, "New Leperino Foods Plant Could Make the Greeley Area Flow with Milk and Money," *Denver Post*, August 27, 2010; Andy Crouch, "Steve Jobs: The Secular Prophet," *Wall Street Journal*, October 8, 2011.

6   Oscar Williams-Grut, "The 15 Most Innovative Countries in the World," *Business Insider*, October 18, 2016; Polly LaBarre, "Who's the Best at Innovating Innovation," *Harvard Business Review*, February 25, 2013; Marx, *Capital,* 163–65.

7   Hillary Clinton's proposed debt forgiveness for entrepreneurs in her 2016 presidential campaign: see Julia Carrie Wong and Danny Yadron, "Hillary Clinton proposes student debt deferral for startup founders," *The Guardian*, June 28, 2016. Since then, FCC officials in the Trump administration moved to repeal the federal regulations of the internet popularly known as "net neutrality"

because they "impeded innovation." Obama-era regulations of predatory for-profit colleges also "created barriers to innovation," according to their critics. In all these cases, we can see how effective the noun's hoary combination of vagueness and virtue can be; calling something "innovative" means you never have to explain why, or how. "Oral Statement of Chairman Ajit Pai," accessed February 27, 2018, https://apps.fcc.gov/edocs_public/attachmatch /DOC-348261A2.pdf; Erica L. Green, "New Higher Education Bill Rolls Back Obama-Era Safeguards," *New York Times*, December 12, 2017.

8   Even the influential management theorist Peter Drucker in *Innovation and Entrepreneurship: Practice and Principles* (New York: Routledge Classics, 2015), 171, was skeptical of the romance of innovation discourse, calling the popular image of the innovator "a cross between Superman and the Knights of the Round Table."

9   Barack Obama alluded to this national spirit in "A Strategy for American Innovation," an economic policy proposal first issued in 2009 and revised periodically during his administration. "America has long been a nation of innovators," the 2015 iteration read. "American scientists, engineers and entrepreneurs invented the microchip, created the internet, invented the smartphone, started the revolution in biotechnology, and sent astronauts to the moon. And America is just getting started." National Economic Council and Office of Science and Technology Policy, "A Strategy for American Innovation: Securing Our Economic Growth and Prosperity" (Washington, DC: The White House, October 2015), 10.

L.

1   Peter Drucker, *Managing for the Future* (New York: Routledge, 1992), 100; Noel Tichy and Ram Charan, "Speed, Simplicity, Self-Confidence: An Interview with Jack Welch," *Harvard Business Review*, September-October 1989, https:// hbr.org/1989/09/speed-simplicity-self-confidence-an-interview-with-jack-welch; Mao Tse Tung, "Quotations from Mao Tse Tung," accessed March 2, 2018, www.marxists.org/reference/archive/mao/works/red-book/ch29.htm.

2   Tim Hindle, *The Economist Guide to Management Ideas and Gurus* (London: Profile Books, 2008), 325. This book's cover features a silhouetted figure in the lotus position. Or take another example: Peter Drucker is described as not just any "guru," but "the one guru to whom other gurus kowtow" in a 1997 *McKinsey Quarterly* profile quoted by Hindle. For other examples of the Orientalist mystification of workaday business as spiritual quest, see "innovation sherpa," "ninja innovators," and surely other phrases I have happily not encountered yet.

3   Business and parenting websites are full of articles on applying the lessons of parenting to the workplace, or conversely on raising children for the

workplace. One example is John Rampton, "15 Tips for Instilling Leadership Skills in Children," *Entrepreneur*, January 23, 2015.

4   Joshua Rothman, "Shut Up and Sit Down, *The New Yorker*, February 29, 2016; Tara Isabella Burton, "Why Are American Colleges Obsessed With 'Leadership'?" *The Atlantic*, January 22, 2014. The top three subject areas at Harvard Business Review Press (https://hbr.org/search?N=0+4294967060) are "leadership and managing people," followed by "managing organizations," and "strategy," the setting of which is a prerogative of leadership.

5   Samuel Smiles, *Men of Invention and Industry* (New York: Harper and Brothers, 1885), 70.

6   As Micki McGee argues, this reversal recapitulated the advice offered to married women at mid-century seeking to escape from the "feminine mystique." Now, finding your "life plan" is a way of "forestalling the contingencies of the economy." *Self-Help, Inc.: Makeover Culture in American Life* (New York: Oxford University Press, 2005), 42.

7   Dale Carnegie, *How to Win Friends and Influence People* (New York: Pocket Books, 1981), 53

8   Beth Blum, "Modernism's Anti-Advice," *Modernism/Modernity* 24, no. 1 (2017): 120.

9   Williams, *Keywords*, 140.

10   Blum, "Modernism's Anti-Advice," 124. A mark of leadership is "the ability to transcend self-doubt," writes Stephen Baum in *What Made Jack Welch Jack Welch: How Ordinary People Become Extraordinary Leaders* (New York: Crown Publishing, 2007), 3.

11   John F. Krafcik, "Triumph of the Lean Production System," *Sloan Management Review* 30, no. 1 (1988), 41–52; James Womack, Daniel T. Jones, and Daniel Roos, *The Machine That Changed the World* (New York: Simon and Schuster, 1990), 13.

12   Womack et al., *The Machine That Changed the World*, 13.

13   John Paul Macduffie, "Workers' Roles in Lean Production: The Implications for Worker Representation," in Steve Babson, ed., *Lean Work: Empowerment and Exploitation in the Global Auto Industry* (Detroit: Wayne State University Press, 1995), 57.

14   Womack et al., *The Machine That Changed the World*, 14; Kim Moody, *Workers in a Lean World: Workers in the International Economy* (New York: Verso Books, 1997), 87.

15   "What is Lean?" Lean Enterprise Institute, accessed February 14, 2018, www.lean.org/WhatsLean/.

M.

1   "The Maker Movement," *Maker Media*, accessed November 28, 2017, https://makermedia.com/maker-movement.

2 Evgeny Morozov, "Making It," *The New Yorker,* January 13, 2014; Dale Dougherty, "The Maker Movement," *Innovations: Technology, Governance, Globalization* 7, no. 3 (2012): 12; The White House: President Barack Obama, "A Nation of Makers," accessed December 3, 2017, https://obamawhitehouse. archives.gov/node/316486; Sarah Boisvert, "Creating the New Collar Workforce," *Make,* May 11, 2018.

3 See Moira Weigel, "Silicon Valley's Sixty-Year Love Affair with the Word 'Tool,'" *The New Yorker,* April 11, 2018.

4 La Berge and Slobodian, "Reading for Neoliberalism, Reading like Neoliberals," 603.

5 Slobodian, *Globalists,* 5–6.

6 "Text of the Communist Party's Platform for the Presidential Election," *New York Times,* August 7, 1948. While the "marketplace of ideas" metaphor is sometimes attributed to John Stuart Mill, John Durham Peters and Edward Nik-Kah offer compelling intellectual histories of the term that situate it in twentieth-century legal and political history and neoliberal economic theories of intellectual freedom, respectively. See Peters, "The 'Marketplace of Ideas': History of the Concept" in Andrew Calabrese and Colin Sparks, eds., *Toward a Political Economy of Culture* (Lanham, MD: Rowman and Littlefield, 2004), 65–81 and Nik-Kah, "What is 'Freedom' in the Marketplace of Ideas?" in Anna Yeatman, ed., *Neoliberalism and The Crisis of Public Institutions: Working Papers in the Human Rights and Public Life Program* (Western Sydney University Whitlam Institute, 2015), 56–69.

7 Marnie Holborow, *Language and Neoliberalism* (London: Routledge, 2015), 52–57; David Graeber, *Towards an Anthropological Theory of Value: The False Coin of Our Own Dreams* (New York: Palgrave, 2001), 15, cited in Holborow.

8 John Peet, *Energy and the Ecological Economics of Sustainability* (Washington, DC: Island Press, 1992), 144.

9 Reed Abelson and Margot Sanger-Katz, "Bipartisan Health Proposal is Too Late for 2018, but a Salve for 2019," *New York Times,* October 19, 2017, on a proposal to calm a "nervous" market; the sullen job market is in Singer, "Universities Race to Nurture Start-Up Founders of the Future."

10 Mirowski, *Never Let a Serious Crisis Go to Waste,* 54–56. As Slobodian writes in "Against the Neoliberalism Taboo," "neoliberalism is a form of regulation, not its radical Other."

11 Michael Young, *The Rise of the Meritocracy* (New Brunswick, NJ: Transaction Publishers, 2011), 11.

12 Michael Young, "Down with Meritocracy," *The Guardian,* June 28, 2001.

13 Stephen J. McNamee and Robert K. Miller Jr., *The Meritocracy Myth* (Lanham, MD: Rowman and Littlefield, 2004); Christopher Hayes, *Twilight of the Elites: America After Meritocracy* (New York: Crown Publishers, 2012), 46; Lauren Berlant, *Cruel Optimism* (Durham, NC: Duke University Press, 2011),

167; on Singapore's meritocracy ideology, see Michael D. Barr and Zlatko Skrbiš, who call it a "ruthless winnowing process" in *Constructing Singapore: Elitism, Ethnicity and the Nation-Building Project* (Copenhagen: NIAS, 2008), 64; Tyler Cowen, *Average Is Over: Powering America Beyond the Age of the Great Stagnation* (New York: Penguin, 2013), 13. On "hyper-meritocracy," see Yuki Honda, *Diversifying Skills and Japanese Society*, cited in Masahiro Abe, "What is at Question in Youth Labour Issues?: The Two Phases of Specialisation, 'Manual-Based' and 'Qualified,'" in Katsuya Minamida and Izumi Tsuji, eds., *Pop Culture and the Everyday in Japan: Sociological Perspectives* (Melbourne: Trans Pacific Press 2012), 256.

N.

1   Jason Read, "As Maine Goes, So Goes the Nation: A Brief Report from the University of Southern Maine," *New APPS: Art, Politics, Philosophy, Science,* March 25, 2014, www.newappsblog.com.

2   Besides the Mother Goose rhyme "Jack Be Nimble," see Douglas English, *A Book of Nimble Beasts: Bunny Rabbit, Squirrel, Toad, and "Those Sort of People"* (Boston: Dana Estes and Co., 1911).

3   Bill Vlasic, "G.M. Chief Expects To Regain Market Share," *New York Times,* January 9, 2013; Micheline Maynard, "US Takes On the Insular G.M. Culture," *New York Times,* June 10, 2009.

4   Talk of the Nation, "Recession Continues To Challenge News Industry," March 15, 2010, www.npr.org.

O.

1   Bruno v. Manno, "Outcome-Based Education: Has it Become More Affliction Than Cure?" *Center of the American Experiment,* August 1, 1994, www .americanexperiment.org/reports-books/outcome-based-education-has-it -become-more-affliction-than-cure/.

2   Trevor Hussey and Patrick Smith, "The Uses of Learning Outcomes," *Teaching in Higher Education* 8, no. 3 (2003): 358

3   Michael Bennett and Jacqueline Brady, "A Radical Critique of the Learning Outcomes Assessment Movement," *Radical Teacher* 94 (Fall 2012): 34–47.

P.

1   Benjamin Franklin, *Autobiography and Other Writings* (New York: Oxford University Press, 1993), 95; David Shumway, *Modern Love: Romance, Intimacy, and the Marriage Crisis* (New York: New York University Press, 2003), 15, 44.

2   "'You've got to find what you love,' Jobs says," *Stanford News,* June 14, 2005, https://news.stanford.edu/2005/06/14/jobs-061505/.

3   Miya Tokumitsu, "In the Name of Love," *Jacobin,* January 12, 2014.

4   Arlie Russell Hochschild, *The Managed Heart: Commercialization of Human Feeling* (Berkeley: University of California Press, 1983), 6–7. Hochschild defines

emotional labor here as that which "requires one to induce or suppress feeling in order to sustain the outward countenance that produces the proper state of mind in others—in this case [of a flight attendant], the sense of being cared for in a convival and safe space."

5   Hochschild, *The Managed Heart*, 37.

6   Paul Slobodzian, "Phoenix is not the place to be for seasoned sports fans," *The State Press*, November 13, 2017; Jeremy Cluff, "Your take on ASU football attendance: Plenty of blame to go around," November 8, 2017, www.azcentral. com; Michael Lewis, "NFL Bandwagon Fans and the Business of Fan Rankings," July 27, 2016, https://scholarblogs.emory.edu/esma/2016/07/27/ nfl-bandwagon-fans-and-the-business-of-fan-rankings/. I am grateful to Jonathan Flatley for his suggestion of passion's "market liminality" and for his living example of passionate fandom.

7   Richard E. Boyatzis, Annie McKee, and Daniel Goleman, "Reawakening Your Passion for Work," *Harvard Business Review*, April 2002.

8   Simone Baribeau, "5 Ways the Obama Campaign was Run like a Lean Startup," *Fast Company*, November 14, 2012; Baribeau, "How Tony Hsieh Pivoted Zappos Into A $1.2 Billion Amazon Acquisition," *Fast Company*, September 4, 2012; Chuck Salter, "Detroit's Bankruptcy Filing Isn't a Fiasco, It's a Pivot," *Fast Company*, July 19, 2013.

9   For example, Emil Lengyel, "Yugoslavia, Key to the Balkans," a review of a book entitled *The Balkan Pivot: Yugoslavia*, *New York Times*, April 7, 1929; "Mozambique's Pivot Toward the West Bringing Few Results," *New York Times*, August 18, 1985.

10   Tracie Mauriello, "Trump looks to refocus presidency in address to Congress," *Pittsburgh Post-Gazette*, February 28, 2018.

R.

1   C. S. Holling, "Resilience and Stability of Ecological Systems," *Annual Review of Ecology and Systematics* 4 (1973): 1–23; F. Berkes, J. Colding, and C. Folke, *Navigating Social-Ecological Systems: Building Resilience for Complexity and Change* (Cambridge: Cambridge University Press, 2003); Carl Folke, "Resilience," Oxford Research Encyclopedia of Environmental Science (Sept. 2016); Charles Perrings, "Resilience and Sustainable Development," *Environment and Development Economics* 11 (2006): 417–427.

2   Jemilah Mamood, "Humanitarian Funding is Not Enough: We Must Increase People's Resilience," *The Guardian*, June 19, 2015 (this article appeared in a section of the newspaper's website, "Global Development," sponsored by the Bill and Melinda Gates Foundation); Julian Reid and Brad Evans, *Resilient Life: The Art of Living Dangerously* (Cambridge: Polity Press, 2014), 81; Linda Graham: *Bouncing Back: Rewiring Your Brain for Maximum Resilience and Well-Being* (San Francisco: New World Library, 2013).

3   International Monetary Fund, "Press Release: Latin America and the Caribbean Should Rebuild Economic Resilience and Flexibility, IMF Says," Press Release 12/150, April 25, 2012; Diane Coutu, "How Resilience Works," *Harvard Business Review* (May 2002).

4   The poster with Washington's quotation has been widely reproduced and discussed: see for example Larry Blumenfeld, "Since the Flood: Scenes from the Fight for New Orleans Jazz Culture," in Eric Weisbard, ed., *Pop When the World Falls Apart: Music in the Shadow of Doubt* (Durham, NC: EMP Museum/Duke University Press, 2012), 174. In *Living a Feminist Life* (Durham, NC: Duke University Press, 2017), 189, Sarah Ahmed writes, "resilience is the requirement to take more pressure; such that the pressure can be gradually increased"; Marco Werman, "Two Years After Earthquake, Symbols of Resilience Sprout in Haiti," *PRI's The World,* July 6, 2012, www.pri.org /stories/2012-07-06/two-years-after-earthquake-symbols-resilience-sprout -haiti; Ben Edwards, "The Most Resilient People on Earth: Haiti Still Standing After Trio of Disasters," *Frontlines*, February/March 2011, www.usaid .gov/news-information/frontlines/haitiwomen-development/most-resilient -people-earth-haiti-still-standing.

5   James Baldwin, "Many Thousands Gone," in *James Baldwin: Collected Essays* (New York: Library of America, 1998), 22.

6   Andrew Zolli and Ann Marie Healy, *Resilience: Why Things Bounce Back* (New York: Simon and Schuster, 2012), 7, 5.

7   Francis Bacon, "Of Anger," *The Works of Francis Bacon, Lord Chancellor of England, vol. 1* (Philadelphia: Carey and Hart, 1842), 60; Thomas De Witt Talmage, *Around the Tea-Table* (London: R. D. Dickinson, 1875), 135.

8   "About Bok," accessed October 10, 2015, www.buildingbok.com; "Become an English Major," Penn State College of the Liberal Arts, English Department, accessed October 9, 2015, english.la.psu.edu/undergraduate; Dave Clarke, "Obama on Iran Deal: 'I expect the debate to be robust,'" *The Washington Post*, July 15, 2015.

9   "Only Robust Teachers for Chicago," *New York Times,* June 16, 1900; Robert Thomas, *The Modern Practice of Physic: Exhibiting the Characters, Causes, Symptoms, Prognostics, Morbid Appearances, and Improved Method of Treating the Diseases of all Climates* (London: Longman, Hurst, Rees, Orme, and Brown, 1816), 30; Carlton McCarthy, *Detailed Minutiae of Soldier Life in the Army of Northern Virginia, 1861–65* (Richmond, VA: B. F. Johnson, 1899), 214.

10   John G. Forrest, "Robust Economy of US Smashes Many Records, Confounds Alarmists," *New York Times,* January 4, 1954; James Hildreth, "After the Budget—What Business Expects," *US News & World Report,* February 22, 1982; David Vance, Twitter post, September 16, 2015, 1:35 pm, https://twitter.com/DVATW; Joanna Rothkopf, "Fox Host: To stop terror recruitment, we need a more "robust, manly" version of Christianity," *Salon*, April 21, 2015.

S.

1   Arun Sundararajan, *The Sharing Economy* (Cambridge, MA: MIT Press, 2016), 27.

2   Niam Yaraghi and Shamika Ravi, "The Current and Future State of the Sharing Economy," Brookings India IMPACT Series No. 032017, March 2017, 6; "Financing 100,000 Entrepreneurs," *Uber Newsroom,* November 25, 2013, www.uber.com/newsroom/financing-100000-entrepreneurs/.

3   Sundararajan, *The Sharing Economy,* 46.

4   Alison Shonkwiler, *The Financial Imaginary: Economic Mystification and the Limits of Realist Fiction* (Minneapolis: University of Minnesota Press, 2017), x–xi.

5   Michael Spence, "The Inexorable Logic of the Sharing Economy," *Project Syndicate,* September 28, 2015, cited in Sundararajan, *The Sharing Economy,* 2014, 204.

6   John Finney, "Guided Bombs Expected To Revolutionize Warfare," *New York Times,* March 18, 1974; Richard Witken, "Accurate 'Smart Bombs' Guided To Objectives by TV or Laser," *New York Times,* May 24, 1972.

7   Perri 6 with Ivan Briscoe, *On the Cards: Privacy, Identity and Trust in the Age of Smart Technologies* (New York: Demos, 1996), 19; John Willman, "Smart House and Home with Technology," *Los Angeles Times,* March 31, 1985.

8   Morozov, *To Save Everything, Click Here: The Folly of Technological Solutionism* (New York: PublicAffairs, 2013), 519.

9   *The New York Times,* May 3, 1987, F45.

10   Evgeny Morozov, *To Save Everything, Click Here* (New York, Public Affairs, 2013), 28.

11   E. Merrick Dodd, Jr., "For Whom Are Corporate Managers Trustees?" *Harvard Law Review,* 45, no. 7 (May 1932): 1145–63

12   One of the most succinct critics is John Argenti, "Stakeholders: The Case Against," *Long Range Planning* 30, no. 3 (1997): 442–45.

13   On Blair's 1996 speech introducing New Labour's "stakeholding" vocabulary, see Norman Fairclough, *New Labour, New Language?* (London: Routledge, 2000), 84–86; Thomas Kaplan, "One Person's 'Special Interest' Is Another's 'Stakeholder,'" March 9, 2011, cityroom.blogs.nytimes.com; for an example of American elites' chiding of China, see Richard Weitz, "As African Presence Grows, China Should Become a Better Stakeholder," Hudson Institute, May 29, 2007, www.hudson.org/research/5190-as-african-presence-grows-china-should -become-a-better-stakeholder.

14   Paul Ingrassia, "Auto Makers Are Sticking With Plans For Aggressive First-Quarter Output," *Wall Street Journal,* January 10, 1986.

15   Elana Fishman, "11 Sustainable Brands That Are Changing The Face Of Eco-Friendly Fashion," *Lucky Shops,* April 22, 2014. Ted Pouls, "Local, Authentic, Sustainable: The Style of The New Artisan Economy," *Pop-Up City,* April 3, 2013.

16   Davies, *The Corpus of Historical American English,* http://corpus.byu.edu/coha/.

17   "Overview:SustainableDevelopment,"WorldBank,accessedDecember11,2015, www.worldbank.org/en/topic/sustainabledevelopment/overview#1.

18   *Our Common Future: The Report of the World Commission on Environment and Development* (New York: Oxford University Press, 1987), 41.

19   "Report of the United Nations Conference on Environment and Development," Rio de Janeiro, 1992, www.un.org/documents/ga/conf151/aconf15126 -1annex1.htm.

20   Paul Burkett, "Marx's Vision of Sustainable Human Development," *Monthly Review* 57, no. 5 (2005); Paul Ehrlich, *The Population Bomb* (New York: Ballantine Books, 1968); Towards Sustainable Mining," The Mining Association of Canada, accessed December 11, 2015, http://mining.ca/towards-sustainable -mining; BP, "Sustainability," accessed December 11, 2015, www.bp.com/en /global/corporate/sustainability.html.

21   Michael Redclift, "The Multiple Dimensions of Sustainable Development," *Geography* 76, no. 1 (1991): 36.

22   Louis Bedigian, "10 Overused Startup Buzzwords," *Forbes,* May 24, 2012.

23   See Daniel Bell, *The Social Sciences Since the Second World War* (New Brunswick: Transaction Publishers, 1985), 4.

24   Steven Johnson, *Where Good Ideas Come From: The Natural History of Innovation* (New York: Penguin, 2010), 17; Jason Headley, "The Innovation of Innovation," accessed March 1, 2016, www.youtube.com/watch?v=jP80EoL4Z70.

25   Calvin Tomkins, "In the Outlaw Era," *The New Yorker,* January 8, 1966.

26   Abraham H. Maslow, "Addition to the Notes on Synergy," *Maslow on Management* (Hoboken, NJ: John Wiley & Sons, 1998), 129.

27   Steve Lohr, "Synergy, Redefined, Back in Style," *New York Times,* May 7, 1989.

T.

1   David Sessions, "The Rise of the Thought Leader," *The New Republic,* June 28, 2017; Patricia Wheatley Burt, *Thought Leadership for Law Firms: After the Legal Services Act* (London: The Law Society, 2011), 53.

2   Joel Kurtzman, "In This Issue," *strategy + business,* accessed March 1, 2018, www.strategy-business.com/article/11895?pg=0; Rev. J. O. M. Hewitt, "The Evolution of Faith," *Free Thought Magazine,* vol XVII (Chicago: 1899), 625; Lyman Abbott, "Henry Ward Beecher," in *Henry Ward Beecher: A Sketch of His Career; with Analyses of His Power as a Preacher, Lecturer, Orator and Journalist, and Incidents and Reminiscences of His Life,* ed. Lyman Abbott (New York: Funk & Wagnalls, 1883), 56; Henry Nehemiah Dodge, *Christus Victor: A Student's Reverie* (New York: G. P. Putnam's Sons, 1900), 37.

3   Shel Israel, "What Makes a Thought Leader?" *Forbes,* March 5, 2012.

W.

1   Halbert L. Dunn, "High-Level Wellness for Man and Society," *American Journal of Public Health* 49, no. 6 (1959): 787–88.

2   The *60 Minutes* segment is preserved at "Wellness Resource Center with Dan Rather on 60 Minutes," accessed March 1, 2018, www.youtube.com/watch?v =LAorj2U7PR4.

3   Lotte Marcus, "Therapy Junkies," *Mother Jones* (March-April 1991), 62.

4   Mehmet Oz, "Real World Wellness," *Oprah.com*, November 6, 2006.

5   Leonard Berry et. al. "What's the Hard Return on Employee Wellness Programs?" *Harvard Business Review*, December 2010.

ACKNOWLEDGMENTS

1   On the innovator as anthropologist, see Jeff Dyer, Hal B. Gregersen, Clayton M. Christensen, *The Innovator's DNA: Mastering the Five Skills of Disruptive Innovators* (Cambridge, MA: Harvard Business Press, 2011), 109; Amanda Lewan, "Quicken Loans Innovates with a 'Small Business' Culture," *Michipreneur*, March 5, 2013; Benjamin Franklin, *Autobiography*, 68.

ABOUT HAYMARKET BOOKS

Haymarket Books is a radical, independent, nonprofit book publisher based in Chicago.

Our mission is to publish books that contribute to struggles for social and economic justice. We strive to make our books a vibrant and organic part of social movements and the education and development of a critical, engaged, international left.

We take inspiration and courage from our namesakes, the Haymarket martyrs, who gave their lives fighting for a better world. Their 1886 struggle for the eight-hour day—which gave us May Day, the international workers' holiday—reminds workers around the world that ordinary people can organize and struggle for their own liberation. These struggles continue today across the globe—struggles against oppression, exploitation, poverty, and war.

Since our founding in 2001, Haymarket Books has published more than five hundred titles. Radically independent, we seek to drive a wedge into the risk-averse world of corporate book publishing. Our authors include Noam Chomsky, Arundhati Roy, Rebecca Solnit, Angela Y. Davis, Howard Zinn, Amy Goodman, Wallace Shawn, Mike Davis, Winona LaDuke, Ilan Pappé, Richard Wolff, Dave Zirin, Keeanga-Yamahtta Taylor, Nick Turse, Dahr Jamail, David Barsamian, Elizabeth Laird, Amira Hass, Mark Steel, Avi Lewis, Naomi Klein, and Neil Davidson. We are also the trade publishers of the acclaimed Historical Materialism Book Series and of Dispatch Books.